MEDIUM ÆVUM MONOGRAPHS
NEW SERIES

MEDIUM ÆVUM MONOGRAPHS
NEW SERIES XVI

TWO LATE MEDIEVAL LOVE TREATISES

Heloise's *Art d'Amour* and a Collection of *Demandes d'Amour*
Edited with Introduction, Notes and Glossary
from British Library Royal MS 16 F II

LESLIE C. BROOK

The Society for the Study of
Mediæval Languages and Literature
1993

The Society for the Study of
Medieval Languages and Literature

http://aevum.space/monographs

ISBN-13:
978-0-907570-09-7 (pb)
978-0-907570-94-3 (ebk)

British Library Cataloguing in Publication Data

A catalogue record for this book
is available from the British Library

First published 1993
This reprint, with updated manuscript images, first issued 2019

Li mestres pert sa poine toute
quant li deciples qui escoute
ne met son cuer el retenir
si qu'il l'en puise sovenir.

(Guillaume de Lorris)

Acknowledgement

The author wishes to acknowledge his grateful thanks to the British Academy for the award of a grant to enable him to publish this monograph.

TABLE OF CONTENTS

PREFACE

I first became aware of the existence of the two treatises on love contained in British Library Royal MS 16 F II some years ago while working on my Bristol Ph.D. thesis on Jean de Meun's translation of the letters of Abelard and Heloise. Following their early twelfth century love affair and their correspondence – which some critics have argued, though never conclusively, was largely a later forgery – mediaeval writers appear to have paid the lovers scant attention. Though allusions to them are few, however, two at least have proved to be eloquent testimony by distinguished writers. It is perhaps principally thanks to Jean de Meun that some aspects of the story of Abelard and Heloise were kept alive, for in his continuation of the *Roman de la Rose* (*c.* 1275), the arguments that Heloise had put to Abelard in order to dissuade him from marrying her are exploited by the surprisingly learned *mari jaloux*, who used them as ammunition against marriage in general; then Villon, who knew his Jean de Meun, made mock of Abelard's plight, which he had brought upon himself through his involvement with Heloise, in his famous *Ballade des Dames du temps jadis*. In neither case is the picture of Heloise a particularly flattering one. Unfairly, she seems to have become for less uninhibited writers than these two something of a *persona non grata*. Christine de Pisan does not find a place for her in her early fifteenth-century *Livre de la Cité des Dames*, and refers to her only in passing and in a disapproving way in her final letter to Pierre Col in the Quarrel of the Rose. So to find Heloise as a *doctor amoris* attached to an adaptation of Andreas Capellanus's *De Amore*, whether with ironic intent originally or not, at least gives us a glimpse of a different kind of reputation, which must have had currency at some time in some scholarly circles; and although the text that I have termed Heloise's *Art d'Amour* is less than perfectly preserved, it certainly deserves to be known.

It was only when I came seriously to work at this text in the British Library MS that I also became interested in the collection of *Minnefragen* which follows it in the MS and forms the second text in this present volume. To call this collection a treatise is open to question, but I believe the use of the term to be justified by the inherently didactic, or partially didactic, nature of the love-questions, and more especially by the didactic intention which I suspect lay behind the inclusion of these questions in this particular MS. In both texts, whether serious or not, love is seen as an absorbing social preoccupation, which requires guidance and precepts, and brings with it problems; and the love-questions fall somewhere between catechism, example, riddle, and problem-page question and answer. There is an essential unity of tone which links the two texts, while the love-questions, relatively modest in number in this MS, belong to a complex nexus of similar questions in other manuscripts, not all of which have yet been fully explored.

The preparation of the two texts for publication has been a slow one. The final version has benefited from the reactions and comments of patient listeners to two conference papers, one on each text, but I was able to put this edition together only thanks to the generosity of the University of Birmingham, which kindly granted me study leave for the Autumn term of 1990. My grateful thanks are also due to the British Library, for providing me with a microfilm of the MS, from which I was able to do most of the work on the actual texts, and for permission to reproduce the two illustrations; to the editors and readers of the Medium Ævum Monograph Series for all their collective encouragement and guidance, and in particular to Dr Elspeth Kennedy and Dr D. G. Pattison; to the British Army, which, in return for two years loss of freedom as a National Serviceman, taught me to touch-type; and especially to my wife and family, who have steadfastly endured not only the clattering of an old portable typewriter, but also, since scholarly activity is never confined to regular hours, my absorption in the project at the expense of time and attention that could otherwise have been given to them.

Leslie C. Brook
June 1992

INTRODUCTION

British Library Royal MS 16 F II is a compilation of texts, beautifully written and richly decorated and illustrated in the Flemish style.[1] The first 137 of its 248 folios contain 165 poems of Charles d'Orléans, including three in English and a short Latin *canticum*.[2] Three other texts then follow, all written in the same hand as the poems: a prose *Art d'Amour*, purporting to be Heloise's instruction of a young pupil called Gaultier (ff. 137–187), a series of *Demandes d'Amour*, consisting of eighteen questions in verse and eighty-eight in prose on points of love (ff. 188–210),[3] and finally a short treatise entitled 'le livre dit grace entiere sur le fait du gouvernment d'un prince', a prosimetrum setting out the qualities and attitudes necessary for good governance (ff. 210–248).[4] Despite the differences in the nature of the texts forming this compilation, there is a clear homogeneity in the cultural ethos and moral attitudes of the aristocratic world which they reflect.

The opening lines of the *Grace entiere* show that this text was copied in 1500 for the benefit of a royal prince, and it is generally and plausibly

[1] For a recent examination of the historical circumstances relevant to this MS and a fuller description of it, see Timothy Hobbs, 'Prosimetrum in *Le Livre dit Grace Entiere sur le fait du gouvernement d'un Prince*, the Governance of a Prince treatise in British Library MS Royal 16 F II', in *Littera et Sensus: Essays on form and meaning in Medieval French Literature presented to John Fox*, edited by D. A. Trotter (University of Exeter, 1989), pp. 49–62. A detailed description of the MS is also to be found in Sir George Warner and Julius Gilson, *Catalogue of Western Manuscripts in the old Royal and King's Collections in the British Museum*, vol. 2 (London, 1921), pp. 203–04; by Francisque Michel in *Collection de documents inédits sur l'histoire de France: Rapports au Ministre* (Paris, 1839), pp. 61–72; and by A. Vallet de Viriville in *Bulletin du Bibliophile*, 7ᵉ série, No. 19 (1846), pp. 839–54.

[2] A selection of these early poems of Charles d'Orléans was edited by John Fox, *Charles d'Orléans: choix de poésies*, éditées d'après le MS Royal 16 F II du British Museum (University of Exeter, 1973).

[3] Edited by Alexander Klein, *Die Altfranzösischen Minnefragen*, Marburger Beiträge zur romanischen Philologie, hg. von Ed. Wechssler, Heft I. (Marburg: Adolf Ebel, 1911), pp. 37–63 and 156–58: see Appendix, pp. 103–107 below.

[4] A short synopsis of this treatise is given by Hobbs, pp. 60–61.

assumed that the whole compilation was put together for the young Prince Arthur, eldest son of the first Tudor monarch, Henry VII, and that the most likely compiler was the prince's tutor, Bernard André, a blind French poet and Augustinian monk.[5] Arthur, Prince of Wales, was born in 1486 and betrothed at the age of three to Catherine of Aragon, who was a year older than he. They corresponded in Latin during their childhood, and were officially married by proxy at Whitsun, 1499. Catherine and Arthur did not actually meet until 1501, when Catherine came to England, and a proper marriage ceremony took place in the November of that year in St Paul's Cathedral. Five months later, on April 2nd, 1502, Arthur died of a virulent infection. His tragic death at the age of fifteen proved historically to be very significant, for the title of Prince of Wales passed to Arthur's younger brother by five years, Henry, who, on the death of his father in 1509, acceded to the throne as Henry VIII. He promptly married Catherine of Aragon, as his father had wished, and had six children by her, of whom only Mary survived infancy. In 1533 Henry divorced Catherine in order to marry Anne Boleyn, using as a pretext Catherine's previous marriage to his elder brother, which he claimed had been consummated, an assertion which Catherine steadfastly denied.[6]

There is ample supporting evidence in the decoration of the six full-page illustrations in the MS to show that it was prepared with the Prince of Wales in mind. Of this decoration Timothy Hobbs writes: 'Recurring images in the borders include greyhounds, dragons, lions, red Lancaster roses, white York roses, and roses symbolically quartered with red and white. The portcullis, symbol of the Tudors, and ostrich feathers, symbol of the Prince of Wales, with his motto "Ic dene", are frequently represented, and almost all the borders include typically Flemish representations of foliage and flowers, birds, butterflies and fruits.'[7] Furthermore John Fox has argued that the poems of Charles d'Orléans chosen for inclusion in this MS are the most appropriate ones for Arthur, separated from his intended loved-one across the sea, as was Charles in exile in England after Agincourt.[8] Likewise the young Arthur would be able to identify with the recipient of the instruction in the *Art d'Amour* and learn

[5] Hobbs (p. 54) expresses some reservations about Bernard André as the possible compiler.

[6] For these historical details I am grateful to Fox (Intro. pp. xvi–xvii) and Hobbs (p. 53).

[7] Hobbs, p. 53.

[8] Fox, Intro. p. xix.

Plate 1: 'Heloise addressing her pupil Gaultier' (Royal MS 16 F II, f° 137r). Reproduced by permission of the British Library.

from the subtleties discussed in the text which follows on various love questions, as well as from the *Grace entiere*, expressly designed for a prince. These treatises, full of medieval wisdom, and with authority and tradition behind them, must have seemed to the compiler as ideal for the young prince to study. If he did study it in depth, however, he would surely have found the first of the love treatises at least rather puzzling.

* * *

No other manuscript of the *Art d'Amour* has ever come to light, and it is the only text in the MS which is written entirely in prose.[9] As with the *Demandes d'Amour*, the first page consists of an appropriate illustration – in this case of the abbess Heloise seated opposite her pupil and addressing him, with a group of ladies listening – and a decorated border which frames the beginning of the text (see Plate 1).[10] Apart from the pictorial clue to its content the text starts with no title, but the opening

[9] Critical attention was first drawn to this *Art d'Amour* by J. Monfrin in the Introduction to his edition of Abelard's *Historia Calamitatum* (Paris: Vrin, 1959), p. 29, n. 46, and the nature of the text was subsequently discussed by Peter Dronke, *Abelard and Heloise in Medieval Testimonies*, W. P. Ker Memorial lecture, 26 (University of Glasgow, 1976), pp. 29–30. He also printed a few extracts from the text in an Appendix, pp. 52–54, under the title *Les epistres de l'abesse Heloys du Paraclit*, following the misleading description of the text in the scribal explicit (f. 187^{v}). A more extensive account of the *Art d'Amour* is to be found in Alfred Karnein, *'De amore' in volkssprachlicher Literatur: Untersuchungen zur Andreas-Capellanus-Rezeption in Mittelalter und Renaissance* (Heidelberg: Winter, 1985), pp. 218–22, and in Leslie C. Brook, 'Un *Art d'Amour* inédit de la fin du moyen âge: son cadre et ses métaphores', in *Courtly Literature: Culture and Context*, edited by Keith Busby and Erik Kooper (Amsterdam–Philadelphia: John Benjamins, 1990), pp. 49–60.

[10] The colouring of the illustration and border is remarkably rich. Heloise is dressed appropriately in black and white, with Gaultier opposite her in a blue-grey cloak, with a yellow and red sleeve to his jacket, a red hat with gold trimmings, a gold chain round his long, brown hair, red and gold hose, and black shoes. He is seated on a green-covered seat under a red canopy trimmed with blue and gold. Of the six courtly ladies on the right of the illustration, one, dressed in grey, gold, and black, appears to be relaying or interpreting Heloise's words to the others. They are dressed in red, gold, or green, with black and gold trimming, and the covering of their heads is also black and gold. The border illustrations are equally rich and varied, and painted on a matt-finish gold background. The initial 'T' of the text is written in gold tracery on a blue background.

paragraph of the treatise hints at the fusion of two traditions:

> Tous ceulx qui ce livre veullent entendre doivent savoir que, quant maistre Pierre Abaielart eut longuement regné et usé de ses arts, sa conscience le reprist. Il fonda une abbaye pres de Sayne, en la terre de Champaigne, que l'en appelle l'abbaye du Paraclit. En celle abbaye du Paraclit fut une nonain esleue abbesse, laquelle eut nom Heloys. Icelle Heloys fut bien introduite en la science des sept arts, et selon l'estat des sept arts elle eut sept graces: c'est assavoir, mauvaises parolles eschiever, mauvaises ouyes fuyr, mauvais voyemens, mauvais contenemens, vivre sans rapine et sans mauvais attouchemens; sur toutes riens elle hayoit luxure. Et pour ce toutes gens qui veulent estre esprouvez en l'art d'Amours et la garder et maintenir doyvent louer l'abbesse Heloys, qui enseigne ung sien disciple, qui Gaultier ot nom.

On the one hand, the reader is presented with an Heloise, experienced, learned, and leading an exemplary life, ideally suited to giving instruction on matters of love to a young pupil, while on the other hand the name of the pupil, Gaultier, given at the end of the paragraph, immediately signals some affinity with Andreas Capellanus's *De Amore*. In fact the reference turns out to be more than a casual memory and borrowing, for although the name does not recur in the treatise, and in spite of the introductory emphasis on Heloise, the *Art d'Amour* is heavily based on Andreas's text. It is fundamentally an adaptation of Book I, chapters 1–6 (Section E) of the *De Amore*, without ever being, in its present state, a close translation of it.

The use of Heloise as instructress and ultimate authority for the precepts set forth in the treatise is, of course, totally foreign to Andreas's text, and represents a development of the tradition, already well established, of the experienced or older woman able to proffer advice on matters of love, such as Lavinia's mother in the *Roman d'Enéas*, or Guinevere and Thessala in *Cligés*, and in more cynical vein, La Vieille in Jean de Meun's part of the *Roman de la Rose*, or La Belle Heaulmière in Villon's *Testament*. In other texts woman's wisdom goes beyond this limited sphere, however, enabling her to give instruction or advice on religious, moral, or social matters, in the figures of the mother in *Le Conte du Graal* and in *Beaudous*, the Dame du Lac in the prose *Lancelot*, or the Dame des Belles Cousines in *Jehan de Saintré*. Sometimes woman's words hint at an awareness of the future, as in the case of the knowledgeable and prophetic cousin and the loathly damsel in *Le Conte du Graal*, or the Demoiselle aux Blanches Mains in *Le Bel Inconnu*, and perhaps all of these portrayals, in their unchallenged authority and mystique, owe not a little to the Sibyls of antiquity.

In a very general sense, of course, and as beings with whom men fall in love, women are the initiators and teachers in romance and in the lyric, making the hero or lover learn of love, inspiring him even when they themselves play only a passive or absent role; while in more active vein Biauté in *Gliglois* deliberately tests the hero's worth through suffering and the proving of self in the tournament reminiscent of Chrétien's 'tournoi de Noauz', and admits it openly to the queen at the end of the text: 'Dame, jou le voel esprover'.[11]

The authority of distinguished courtly ladies to pronounce on questions of love is recognized by Andreas himself, when at one point he refers a dispute on the crucial issues of whether love can exist in marriage, and whether jealousy between lovers is acceptable, to no less a person than Marie de Champagne (Book I, chapter 6, Section G); and in Book II a series of judgments on love problems is given either by Marie de Champagne, or by Queen Eleanor, Ermangarde of Narbonne, the Countess of Flanders, or a court of ladies in Gascony.

In the structure superimposed in the *Art d'Amour* on the early part of Andreas's treatise, Heloise is placed on a par with these court personages, and her role is as disinterested as was theirs. Although there is no other example in the legend of Heloise of her playing such a role,[12] the author clearly considered that her wisdom and experience fitted her for the task. Her presumed qualifications probably stemmed originally from the literary fame she achieved as a result of her arguments against marriage, which Abelard reported in his autobiographical *Historia Calamitatum*, and which earned her the cynical admiration of Jean de Meun for her intelligence, and led Villon to refer to her as 'tres saige'.[13] Yet in the introductory paragraph of the *Art d'Amour* her actual credentials make no such direct or specific reference, mentioning only generalized, depersonalized attitudes. Nevertheless, the writer responsible for adding her name to the treatise probably knew of her principally from the *Roman de la Rose*, though the allusions in this same opening paragraph presuppose some familiarity with the Correspondence of Abelard and Heloise, and in

[11] *Gliglois*, edited by Charles H. Livingston (Cambridge, Mass.: Harvard U.P., 1932), v. 2798.

[12] See Charlotte Charrier, *Héloïse dans l'histoire et dans la légende* (Paris: Champion, 1933).

[13] Guillaume de Lorris et Jean de Meun, *Le Roman de la Rose*, edited by F. Lecoy, 3 vols. (Paris: Champion, 1965–70), vv. 8729–8802; and Villon, *Ballade des Dames du temps jadis*, second stanza.

particular with the *Historia Calamitatum*, the letter which prompted the exchange between the former lovers. The scribe, certainly, knew of the existence of the Correspondence, for beneath the end of the text he wrote: 'Cy finent les epistres de l'abesse Heloys du Paraclit, laquelle abaÿe maistre Pierre Abaielart fonda ainçois qu'il mourust' (f. 187v), unless he was merely relying on Jean de Meun's reference in the *Roman de le Rose* to 'ses espitres'.[14]

By limiting itself to approximately only half of Book I of the *De Amore*, and therefore to about one quarter of the complete text of Andreas, the French treatise echoes only that part of its Latin predecessor which deals with the nature of love and how to attain it. It reaches a convenient stopping point, however, with the story of the visit to the 'verger d'amour', an allegorical presentation of the rewards or punishments granted to women in an after-life in accordance with their response to love.

When the *Art d'Amour* is compared with the relevant part of the *De Amore* there are three levels on which it can be seen to differ from Andreas's work:

(i) The general framework of the text, in respect of the identity of the speakers in the dialogues or the authority for particular statements;
(ii) The order and consistency with which statements and topics in Andreas's treatise are dealt with in the *Art d'Amour*;
(iii) The treatment of comparable points, which on the whole bear only an approximate relationship to the Latin treatise.

The *Art d'Amour* will now be examined from these three standpoints.

(i) The framework of the text and the role of Heloise

Any expectations that the reader may have had from the opening paragraph that Heloise might play a substantial role in the ensuing text are quickly dashed. It soon becomes apparent that her role is nominal, and that basically it has been superimposed on the precepts derived from the *De Amore* by the use of introductory formulae, such as: 'L'abbesse Heloys monstre a son disciple par certaines raisons comment povres amans ...' (f. 139r), 'L'abbesse Heloys demonstre et si enseigne a son disciple qu'il garde que ...' (f. 139r), or 'L'abbesse Heloys du Paraclit cy enseigne et demonstre a son disciple que ...' (f. 140v). She is referred to either by name or by the title 'abbesse' sixty-two times overall, in similar formulae or in simple

[14] vv. 8783–86.

intercalated clauses, such as: 'dit l'abesse Heloys' (f. 161^{r}), and 'ce dit Heloys' (f. 161^{v}). At times the supposed transmission of instruction from teacher to specific pupil is forgotten in introductory formulae such as: 'Et demonstre l'abbesse Heloys du Paraclit que ...' (f. 141^{r}), 'L'abbesse Heloys demonstre et si enseigne que ...' (f. 141^{v}), or 'Et pour ce dit l'abesse Heloys que ...' (f. 148^{r}); or the pupil is replaced by 'nous': 'L'abbesse Heloys nous demonstre que ...' (f. 143^{r}), and 'Ce nous demonstre l'abesse Heloys que ...' (f. 158^{r}). Heloise's role is, then, only a reported one, except that at one stage direct speech is employed: 'Je, Heloys, abesse du Paraclit, pour nulle riens ne me departiroye de la doctrine de mon disciple' (f. 161^{r}), and a few lines below, 'Et pour ce prie je Dieu, dit l'abesse Heloys ...' (f. 161^{r}). Overall the references to Heloise seem to be scattered arbitrarily throughout the text, but the writer is dogged in his reattribution of Andreas's material to her authority, and her final task is to introduce the visit to the 'verger d'amour': 'L'abesse Heloys demonstre au sien disciple que une dame estoit de trop noble semblance ...' (f. 183^{r}).

That Heloise's authority has been added to a pre-existing set of precepts can be illustrated by the fact that at times the text continues independently of her, with precepts attributed to 'la rigle d'amours', or introduced by a formula indicating some kind of discussion between 'l'amant' and 'l'amante'. A good example of this occurs in the passage beginning at the bottom of f. 151^{r} and continuing to f. 152^{v}. It starts as follows: 'Et pour ces choses devant dictes et celles qui sont ensuivant demonstre Heloys l'abbesse a son disciple que ...', but then the next three sentences begin: 'La rigle d'amours demonstre par droite raison que ...', 'La rigle d'amour nous enseigne que ...' and 'La rigle d'amours demonstre que ...'; after which there is a sequence of statements introduced by 'L'amant dit a l'amante que ...' or simply 'L'amant dit que ...', until there is a return to 'La rigle d'amours demonstre que ...' (bottom of f. 152^{r}), and eventually to 'L'abbesse Heloys demonstre et enseigne a son disciple que ...' (f. 152^{v}). Even if in this passage, which is followed by another similar one, Heloise is considered as introducing what 'la rigle d'amour' or 'l'amant' say, she is momentarily eclipsed by the text, which continues without her. In a much longer passage, beginning at the bottom of f. 164^{v}, Heloise is again eclipsed, after introducing a discussion between 'l'amant' and 'l'amante':

> L'abbesse Heloys demonstre et enseigne a son disciple comment l'amant doit respondre a l'amante, et selon les choses proposees. L'amant dit qu'il fait ... Et dit l'amante a l'amant: tu m'admonnestes ... (ff. 164^{v}–165^{r});

and in the midst of the ensuing discussion, adding to the confusion of the narrative perspective of the text, 'l'amant' requests instruction from 'l'amante':

> Et par ceste raison, dit l'amant a l'amante, que je te voye introduicte en l'art d'amours, je requier ta grace et que [par] ta doctrine me veuilles enseigner et ce qui est couvenable aux commandemens d'amours, et tout ce qui affiert a porter les armes d'amours ... (f. 167^{v}).

The use of the terms 'l'amant' and 'l'amante' is in itself a modification of Andreas's treatise. In his long chapter 6 (Book I), entitled 'Qualiter amor acquiratur et quot modis' ('How love is won, and in how many ways'),[15] Andreas had set up a series of dialogues between the following pairs:

Dialogue	A: commoner and common woman	(§§21–67)[16]
"	B: commoner and noble lady	(§§68–115)
"	C: commoner and lady of higher nobility	(§§116–165)
"	D: nobleman and common woman	(§§166–195)
"	E: nobleman and noblewoman	(§§196–280)
"	F: higher nobleman and common girl	
"	G: higher nobleman and noblewoman	
"	H: higher nobleman and higher noblewoman	

The French treatise breaks off before the end of Dialogue E. From the table given in (ii) below it will be seen that the opening of Dialogue A, which would identify the speakers of that Dialogue, is not found in the *Art d'Amour*. For the other dialogues, however, the opening relates closely to Andreas:

Dialogue B: 'Se aucun amant de bas lieu requiert noble dame ou damoyselle de noble et hault parentaige ...' (f. 146^{v})

Dialogue C: 'Il couvient, ce dit Heloys, que quant [l']amant est nez du peuple et de bas lieu, et il se veult ingerer d'aymer noble personne ...' (f. 161^{v})

Dialogue D: 'L'abesse Heloys demonstre et si enseigne a son disciple que, se l'amant noble requiert l'amour de femme qui soit du peuple ...' (f. 172^{v})

Dialogue E: 'L'abesse Heloys demonstre et enseigne a son disciple que, s'aucun noble amant requiert l'amour d'aucune noble dame ...' (f. 179^{r}).

In spite of this, these initial identities are not carefully maintained through-

[15] All quotations from the *De Amore* and the English translation of the Latin are taken from P. G. Walsh, *Andreas Capellanus on Love* (London: Duckworth, 1982).

[16] These convenient sub-divisions of the Latin text are taken from Walsh's edition.

out the ensuing dialogues. For a start, after the introduction of the relevant social standing of each interlocutor, the discussion in all of Andreas's dialogues is punctuated by 'Homo ait' or 'Mulier ait' prefacing each speaker's remarks. In the *Art d'Amour* this invariably becomes 'l'amant (dit)' and 'l'amante (dit)', thus crucially altering the relationship between the speakers. The change is most noticeable, of course, in those parts of the treatise where there is otherwise an identifiable resemblance between the arguments of the *De Amore* and the *Art d'Amour*; but because of the lexical similarity between the two words, it is scarcely surprising to find that at times points made in the *De Amore* by the man, are made by the woman, or vice-versa, in the French treatise, e.g. 'ja soit ce, dit l'amante a l'amant' (f. 160v, cf. *De Amore*, §114), and 'L'amant dit a l'amante qu'il appartient au faucon ...' (f. 153r, cf. *De Amore*, §82). The risk of this occurring is increased by the greater frequency of such attributions in the French text than in the Latin; for instance, in the passage beginning 'Dit aussi l'amante a l'amant que l'ordonnement ...' (f. 163v) and ending '... moult de perilz' (f. 164v), which corresponds to one speech in Andreas's treatise introduced by 'Mulier ait', there is a total of six references to the speakers, in five of which 'l'amante' addresses 'l'amant', but in one it is the opposite: while immediately preceding this passage, a speech which should be by the man is attributed three times to the woman: 'Et pour ce dit l'amante a l'amant ...', etc. (f. 163r). On f. 166r, because there is no indication of a change of speaker, the sentence beginning 'Car quant la prouesse ...' is presumably attributed to 'l'amant', as a continuation of his speech, whereas in Andreas (§138) it is said by the woman. Again at 172r, the sentence beginning 'Et pour ce ...' looks like a continuation of the preceding speech, instead of marking the start of the man's speech (Andreas, §162).

Even more confusingly in the case of Dialogue D between the nobleman and the common woman ('Nobilis plebeiae'), the correct relationship established at the beginning of dialogue (f. 172v) is completely upset on the verso of the next folio by the insertion of the following introductory statement: 'Adoncques l'amant qui est nez du bas peuple doit arraisonner la noble amante courtoysement ...' (f. 173v). This reversal is then reinforced a few lines further on with: 'Et la noble amante respont ainsi ...', 'Et en ceste maniere respont la noble amante ...', and 'Lors la noble amante respont ...' (f. 174r). A further transformation then occurs in respect of Andreas's simple 'Homo ait' (§173), which is replaced by 'La rigle d'amours sy demonstre au messaiger d'amours que ...' (f. 174r). This new role, which originates in the remark by 'l'amant' (f. 173^{v}) that he is 'messagier de la chevallerie d'amours' (cf. Andreas, §169: 'Nuntius sum quidem vobis ab amoris aula transmissus' ["I have been sent over as messenger to you from the court of Love"]), is maintained, with some variation, throughout the dialogue, although the discussion for a while turns on references by both interlocutors to 'l'amante du peuple' (ff. 174^{v}, 175^{r}–175^{v}, etc.), which, given the circumstances already described, can have only a theoretical application to their discussion, e.g. 'A ce respont la noble amante au messager d'amours que quant l'amante du peuple ...' (f. 176^{v}). And since the original roles have been reversed, it is not surprising to find that after a while speeches are also attributed to the 'wrong' speaker. Thus, on f. 176^{r} 'Homo ait' (§177) is replaced by 'La noble amante respont ... que ...', and the reply ('Mulier ait', §179) is replaced by 'Le messager d'amours respont ... que ...' At the end of this sentence the allusion to 'l'amant du peuple' also represents a change of sex from Andreas's 'plebeiae mulieris' (§179), and gender reversal occurs too in the remark that follows: 'Ne elle ne prent pas nom de noble dame ...'. When we reach f. 177^{r} (Andreas, §184) the 'correct' gender of the interlocutors in the discussion is temporarily restored, but the sheer complexity of the construct in the French treatise by this point can be seen by the introductory statement: 'L'abesse Heloys demonstre a son disciple comment il doit respondre aux argumens du messager d'amours. Ja soit ce, dit le messagier ...' (cf. Andreas: 'Homo ait: Quamvis ...'). Then as the sentence proceeds the speaker is changed to 'le disciple', and the general sense of hopeless confusion reigns until the close of the dialogue (f. 179^{r}), with 'l'amant' replying to 'l'amante' within what should be the woman's speech (f. 177^{v}), 'le disciple' standing in for 'Homo ait' (f. 178^{r}), and the man's reply in §193 (f. 178^{v}) changing from 'Homo ait: Consilium tibi denegare non possum' ('The man says: I cannot refuse you deliberation') to 'Le messager d'amours respont au disciple de l'abbesse Heloys et lui demonstre par droit d'amours que il ne lui puet donner conseil'! Again 'l'amant respont a l'amante' within the woman's speech (f. 178^{v}, §194), and 'l'amant respont' (f. 179^{r}, §195) in place of the woman. It should be noted, too, that amid this attribution of remarks, the social differentation between commoner and noble is totally lost, the last reference to 'la noble amante' being on f. 176^{v}.

With the advent of Dialogue E (f. 179^{r} et seq.) some kind of order is re-established in the attributions, the discussions now being between a 'noble amant' and a 'noble amante', except that between ff. 181^{r} and 182^{v} the speeches are mostly attributed to the 'wrong' person, designated simply as 'l'amant' or 'l'amante'. Finally the closing story of the visit to the 'verger d'amour' changes the first-person narrative of the squire ('armiger') in Andreas, to a third-person one, the story-teller being referred to as 'le messagier' (f. 183^{v} et seq.), or even 'le chevallier messager' (f. 185^{v}).

(ii) The De Amore *and the* Art d'Amour*: distribution of comparable text*

It is not possible to relate every sentence or paragraph of the French treatise to an identifiable equivalent section in Andreas's *De Amore*. In (iii) below it will be demonstrated that there is usually only an approximate affinity, with sometimes a tenuous link and considerable modification, or merely a vague reminiscence. However, the table below shows the distribution throughout the pages of the *Art d'Amour* of material derived from the *De Amore*, in so far as it can be traced. The sign [] indicates that a passage in the French text has no traceable equivalent in Andreas's treatise. Where appropriate, Dialogues A–E are shown alongside chapter 6 of the *De Amore.*

	Chapters in *De Amore*, Book I (with sub-divisions, Walsh edition)	MS 16 F II
	1 §§ 1–7	138^{r}–139^{r}
	2 § 7?	139^{r}
	6 §§ 8–17, 23 [] 24–5	139^{r}–141^{r}
	5 §§ 2–3	141^{r}
	6 § 1	141^{v}
	5 §§ 4–8	141^{v}–142^{r}
	6 §§ 1–8	142^{r}–143^{r}
	1 §§ 8–10	143^{r}–143^{v}
	1 § 8	144^{r}
	2 §§ 1 [] 2 [] 6	144^{r}–144^{v}
	3 § 1	144^{v}
	4 § 1	144^{v}
	5 §§ 1 [] 3	144^{v}–145^{r}
A–B	6 §§ 55–56, 60, 68–71	145^{v}–147^{v}
A	6 § 45	147^{v}
	[]	147^{v}–149^{r}
A	6 §§ 43 (56?)	149^{r}
B	6 § 69	149^{v}
	[]	149^{v}–150^{r}
A	6 § 37	150^{r}

	[]	150ʳ–150ᵛ
A	6 §§ 41–43	150ᵛ–151ʳ
	[]	151ᵛ–152ᵛ
	1 § 7	152ᵛ
	[]	152ᵛ–153ʳ
B	6 §§ 80–91	153ʳ–155ʳ
	[]	155ʳ–155ᵛ
B	6 § 95	155ᵛ
	[]	155ᵛ–156ᵛ
B	6 §§ 98–115	156ᵛ–161ʳ
C	6 § 116	161ᵛ
	[]	161ᵛ–162ʳ
C	6 § 119	162ʳ
B	6 § 72	162ᵛ
C	6 §§ 121–165	162ᵛ–172ᵛ
D	6 §§ 166–179	172ᵛ–176ᵛ
D	6 §§ 183–184	176ᵛ–177ʳ
D	6 §§ 188–195	177ʳ–179ʳ
E	6 §§ 196–222	179ʳ–183ᵛ
E	6 §§ 237–254	183ᵛ–186ʳ
E	6 §§ 259–266	186ʳ–187ᵛ
E	6 § 273	187ᵛ

Three points are clear from this table:

(a) In relation to Andreas's *De Amore* the text is a muddle, jumping wildly, particularly in the first seven folios, from chapter to chapter, but settling down more from f. 145ᵛ onwards, although continuous sequences of Andreas's text really occur only from f. 156ᵛ onwards.

(b) Even where continuous comparison is possible on a substantial scale, notably from f. 162ᵛ, there are sizeable omissions:
§§180–182, representing a complete reply by the man;
§§185–187, a substantial portion of a speech by the man;
§§223–236, an important section of text concerning the various types of women who inhabit the different doorways of the palace of love, and the start of the man's story which forms the closing episode of the *Art d'Amour*, the visit to the 'verger d'amour'. Because of this latter omission the reader of the French treatise is deprived of the background which would help explain why the lady is riding a scraggy horse, and why the squire ('messagier' in the *Art d'Amour*) is seeking his lord;
§§255–258, a description of two important areas allotted to groups of women according to their deserts, *humiditas* and *siccitas*. This consider-

ably diminishes the impression of the overall description of the 'verger d'amour';

§§267–272, containing the precepts of love given by the king of love.

(c) There are several isolated pages of text in the French treatise which cannot be related directly to the *De Amore*, although the precepts on these pages are similar in nature to the rest of the text. Should this be attributed to free development within the French treatise, or to another source?

(iii) A close comparison of comparable passages

The French treatise can in no way be considered to be, or even perhaps ever to have been, a close translation of Andreas's *De Amore*. Even in those sections, in chapter 6 for instance, where it follows the sequence of argument with some degree of recognizability, it appears to be no more than a rough adaptation. A comparison between the Latin text of chapter 6, §133 and its French counterpart provides a good illustration of the way that the text has been modified:

> Homo ait: Fateor quod amari posco, qui dulcior quam sit in orbe vita est in amore vivere. Sed verba vestra manifeste demonstrant quod me recusatis amare et hoc propter inferioris ordinis vilitatem, quamvis in multa constituar probitate (6, §133). (The man says: I grant that I am asking for your love, because living in love is sweeter than any form of life on earth. But your comment clearly shows that you refuse me your love, your reason being the worthlessness of my lower rank, in spite of my abundant integrity.)

> L'abbesse Heloys demonstre et enseigne a son disciple comment l'amant doit respondre a l'amante, et selon les choses proposees. L'amant dit qu'il fait ce que amours lui admonneste, car il n'est plus doulce chose en ce monde que vivre en bonne amour. Et dit l'amante a l'amant: tu m'admonnestes par tes parolles que tu refuses l'amour de moy. Je apperçoy bien pourquoy c'est. C'est pour la vile chose qui est dicte luxure, ja soit ce que je soye renommee de prouesse (ff. 164^v–165^r):

or again a few pages further on:

> Sed id quod de intenso et remisso mihi crure opposuistis ac pede prolixo, non multum de ratione procedit. Fertur etenim quendam in Italiae finibus degere comitem habentem subtilia crura et ab optimis parentibus derivatum et in sacro palatio clarissima dignitate pollentibus omnique decoris specie coruscantem, cunctisque fertur abundare rerum divitiis, omni tamen probitate, ut dicitur, destitutus est, omnesque ipsum boni mores ornare verentur, pravique omnes dicuntur in eo domicilium invenisse (6, §142). (Your objections to my bulging flabby legs and big feet are not securely grounded. We are told that within the boundaries of Italy dwells a count

with slender legs, the son of the best of parents who are accorded the most distinguished rank in the sacred palace. He is radiant with every mark of beauty: he is said to be endowed with all manner of riches. But rumour has it that he is wholly lacking in integrity, all good manners are reluctant to embellish him, and all debased habits have reportedly found a home in him.)

Et par ceste raison monstre l'amant a l'amante qu'elle le reprent a tort. L'en treuve, dit l'amant, que aucunesfois es parties de France ung conte est trouvé riche de grans possessions et de grans rentes, et mal taillié de corps et mal fait de membres, et chascun l'onnoure et lui obeyst. Et est advis a tous qu'il n'ait point de prouesse, et par droit jugement les meurs de celles gens sont trouvees mauvaises, et ont fait leur nyc au coing de leur maison (f. 167[r]).

The original argument or movement of thought can be completely distorted, as for example in the discussion which is supposed to be between the commoner and the noble lady. At one point the man's reply begins as follows:

Homo ait: Quod mihi benignum et suave praestitistis responsum, multum in hoc vestra probitas denotatur, quia vestrae voluistis naturae consulere, ac vestra verba generi convenire. Nihil enim magis generosae personae potest congruere laudibus quam si in suis dictis dulci sermone fruatur, et nulla videntur magis nobili contraire generi et sanguinis nobilitati detrahere quam aspera et inurbana verba proferre. Quod autem dixistis meam faciem vobis esse cum genere manifestam, vehementer admiror quia vestram video in hoc errare prudentiam, quum illis videamini erratibus assentire, qui morum probitatem sine genere ac forma reiiciunt et formae venustatem ac sanguinem generosum sine omni probitate recipiunt (6, §§89–90). (The man says: Your kind and gentle reply abundantly reveals your moral worth, for you sought to indulge your nature and to fit your words to your noble birth. Nothing can be more conducive to the praise of a noblewoman than her employment of gentle language when she speaks, and nothing more clearly contradicts noble birth and noble blood than harsh and discourteous utterance. But your comment that my appearance and my birth are together obvious to you causes me considerable surprise, for I observe that your wisdom is greatly mistaken on this point. You appear to consent to the false attitudes that reject moral worth if it is not applied to family and beauty, and that accept a handsome appearance and noble blood without a scrap of moral worth.)

Tout amant doit savoir comment il doit respondre aux choses qui appartiennent a l'art d'amer. Le disciple d'amours doit louer la science de son maistre, le sens, le loz, et la prouesse, et la grant plenté de bonnes meurs; car les maistres scevent conseiller a l'art de nature, et conjoindre et amener les commandemens d'amours a droit. Nulle chose ne peut plus plaire aux nobles amantes que ce qu'elles soient arraisonnees par doulces

> parolles et de bons faits et de bons ditz et de bons contenemens de leurs amys. Cy dit encore la rigle d'amours que nulle chose n'est plus griefve a nobles personnes que parolles griefves et aspres a ouyr de ceulx de son lignaige ou de sa noblesse. A ce la rigle d'amours se merveille moult que les personnes des nobles amans si se prennent a louer leur fourme et leur beaulté, ou leur prouesse ou leur lignage (ff. 154ᵛ–155ʳ).

There are nevertheless moments when the French treatise follows Andreas more closely, as can be seen in the following passage. It will be noted, though, that the setting ('Homo ait' – 'Mulier ait') has been partially altered, and there is a tendency for some free elaboration of the Latin text:

> Homo ait: Quamvis nolim tuos sermones arguere, nulla tamen possum ratione videre, si plebeius nobilem in probitate transcendat, quare ipsum non debeat in suscipiendis superare muneribus, quum ab eodem Adam stipite derivemur. Mulier ait: Melius in mensa regia sedet aurum quam in pauperis domo vel rusticano tugurio, et longe honorabilius trotonerius et macer equitatur equus quam pinguis valde et opimae et suavis ambulaturae asinus. A tuis ergo resipisce erroribus et aliis haec sumenda relinque (6, §§112–113). (The man says: I do not wish to refute your words, but I see no reason why a commoner who is superior in character to a nobleman should not rise above him in the gifts which he receives. For we are all sprung from the same stock in Adam. The woman says: A king's table is a better setting for gold than is the home of a pauper or the hut of a farmhand. A seat on a scraggy trotting-horse is better than one on the plumpest ass with the smoothest gait. So learn a lesson from your mistakes, and leave such prizes for others to attain.)
>
> Et pour ce que l'amante ne veult pas reprendre les moles parolles de l'amant, elle demonstre par raison que, se ung homme du peuple, plain de bonnes meurs, puet surmonter par sa grace l'amant qui est né de noble lieu, pourquoy ne pourra icellui du peuple, par ses dons pris et receuz, et ses traveilz aussi souffers, estre receu en la court d'amours par le jugement de la vraye amante? Car tous amans sont nez et sont du lignaige d'Eve et d'Adam, ja soit ce que l'or et l'argent soit mieulx seant en la court d'un roy qu'en la court d'un vilain de ville champestre. L'amante preuve par vray argument d'amour que le maisgre roncin trottant porte plus souef une longue voye que l'asne qui est gras et bien amblant. Pour ce dit l'amante a l'amant qu'il se prengne garde a ceste comparoison (ff. 160ʳ–160ᵛ).

In spite of such passages, the distance between the *De Amore* and the *Art d'Amour* can lead to obscurities which compound those caused by the kind of omission referred to in (ii) (b) above: in the section of text corresponding to Andreas, 6, §§215–222, for instance, it is no longer clear that it is the woman who is doing the rejecting, and thereby will suffer (ff. 182ʳ–183ʳ).

* * *

It follows from the foregoing analysis that the French treatise must have some character of its own, and it would be a mistake merely to look at it somewhat negatively as a poor and muddled adaptation of the *De Amore*. For a start, to do so could obscure any speculation as to how the text in its present state might have come into being. At what stage did the blend of Andreas and Heloise take place? Perhaps the present treatise started life as a prose translation of the relevant part, or even of the whole, of the *De Amore*, of which the opposition 'amant'/'amante', despite careless and confusing attribution, is a vestige. After some deformation Heloise's role may have been added (late thirteenth century onwards?), once the text was no longer recognizable as a version of Andreas's treatise, or the thrust of the original arguments was lost, and when 'la rigle d'amour' had already assumed considerable authority over the latter part of the text. At any event a statement such as the following is meaningless in the present version of the French treatise, but it did make sense in Andreas (see note to text): 'L'abbesse Heloys si demonstre et enseigne a son demourant en sa discipline que par ces choses devant dictes il pert toute sa paine et si traveille en vain' (f. 154[v]). Had it already lost meaning before the intervention of Heloise, or did the addition of her name and authority cause the loss of meaning?

The question then really is this: did the French treatise ever exist as a modification of the *De Amore* and make more sense than the version preserved in Royal MS 16 F II does, with or without the inclusion of Heloise? The evidence of passages of independent development (e.g. between ff. 147[v] and 149[r]) shows that it is not just a garbled adaptation of Andreas. Moreover, adaptation can have a positive side, and indicate deliberate substitution, as in the case of the four degrees of love (ff. 146[r]–146[v]; see note to text). Elsewhere, though, there are some rather superficial, even fatuous or ill-expressed statements, such as the following: 'Nul homme ne peult faire nul bien se l'admonnestement d'amour ne luy admonneste' (f. 148[v]); and sometimes statements are difficult to understand: 'Lesquelles choses tous amans doivent faire a cause de pure deité' (ibid.). On the whole the text is rather flat; it can be confusing, obscure, and repetitious, often little more than a series of non-sequiturs and aphorisms, or a sequence of only loosely connected statements (e.g. f. 151[v]). Although the text has been set out by the scribe in paragraphs, no headings divide it up to show that he was aware of the original divisions in Andreas. Furthermore, the essentially adulterous nature of love as expounded by Andreas is not really apparent, partly because of the rather muddled state of the French text, but partly because those sections of Andreas in which this is most clearly stated, such as in the reply by the Countess of Champagne to the letter addressed to her, occur further on in the Latin treatise than the part covered by the *Art d'Amour.*[17] Likewise the absence of any of the material from Book III of Andreas's treatise, which is entitled *De reprobatione amoris* and functions as a palinode, eliminates any possibility of retrospective ironic interpretation of the French version in its present form. Unhindered by doubts, the reader can thus take the chosen portion of Andreas's treatise as a serious text, whatever the original intention of Andreas might have been.[18] Heloise, too, is used in a way which reinforces the seriousness of the French text, while adding, perhaps, to its blandness. There is no reference to her anti-marriage reputation, which had been highlighted by Jean de Meun; instead she is portrayed simply as an expert able to dispense general advice on the attainment and nature of love, with no trace of cynicism. Looked at positively, in fact, the text has undeniable qualities: it presents throughout the aristocratic values of *courtoisie*, with constant insistence on the pri-

[17] Walsh, I, 6, Dialogue G, §§395–400 (pp. 155–57). The general discussion on love and marriage, and on the married state of the lady being petitioned, begins a little before this, §366 (p. 147). The adulterous nature of the love being sought is also clear in Dialogue F §294 (p. 125), Dialogue G §364 (p. 145) and Dialogue H §§443–44 (p. 171).

[18] Modern ironic interpretations of the *De Amore* stem from the work of D. W. Robertson, Jr: 'The Doctrine of Charity in Mediaeval Literary Gardens: A Topical Approach through Symbolism and Allegory', *Speculum*, 26 (1951), 24–49; 'The Subject of the *De amore* of Andreas Capellanus', *Modern Philology*, 50 (1952–3), 145–61; and especially *A Preface to Chaucer* (Princeton University Press, 1962). See also Alfred Karnein, *'De amore' in volkssprachlicher Literatur ...* For more extreme ironic interpretations, see Betsy Bowden, 'The Art of Courtly Copulation', *Medievalia et Humanistica*, 9 (1979), 67–85; Hubert Silvestre, 'Du nouveau sur André le Chapelain', *Revue du moyen âge latin*, 36 (1980), 99–106; and Bruno Roy, 'André le Chapelain, ou l'obscénité rendue courtoise', in *Mittelalterbilder aus neuer Perspektive*, ed. Ernstpeter Ruhe and Rudolf Behrens (Munich: Fink, 1985), pp. 59–74. An excellent analysis of the various ironic views is to be found in Don A. Monson, 'Andreas Capellanus and the Problem of Irony', *Speculum*, 63 (1988), 539–72.

macy of 'bonnes meurs'; it is surprisingly rich in courtly imagery,[19] while enough survives of the 'verger d'amour' episode to display a talent for evocation and description, and an awareness that love is an essential part of life, and not just a worldly game.

It is impossible for us to know whether the scribe was copying from a better version of the treatise, but it cannot have been scrupulously checked after copying, otherwise the meaningless repetition (ff. 180^r–180^v) would not have been allowed to stand.[20] Of all the texts contained in Royal MS 16 F II this one seems to have been the worst served by copying, although this may be because no better copy was available to the compiler. What, then, was poor Prince Arthur meant to make of it all? Was he really intended to study it closely, or was it felt that, despite its obscurities, there was enough clear, good advice in aphoristic form to provide the young prince with some idea of attitudes and behaviour to adopt? Was it therefore intended for browsing or casual reference, rather than for close reading? Or, dare one suggest, was prestige of ownership more important than content? What is rather puzzling to the modern reader is the contrast in quality between the text and the exquisite illustration at the head of it. As for the text itself, it is hard to escape the conclusion that at one time it was probably longer, covering all the sections of the *De Amore* up to Dialogue E at least, and in their proper order.

* * *

Curiously there is a conscious or merely coincidental echo of Andreas's treatise in the idea of following this *Art d'Amour* in Royal MS 16 F II with a series of *Demandes d'Amour*, the title given to this collection of questions and answers by the scribe himself at the beginning and end of the text; for in Book Two of the *De Amore*, as has been mentioned above, there occurs a series of judgments on love problems, though their content is not the same as in the *Demandes d'Amour*. Nevertheless, historically and culturally there is undeniably some relationship between these *Demandes d'Amour* and the kind of judgments given by the distinguished ladies to whom problems were submitted in the *De Amore*. In fact, there is an even closer but less readily noticeable link between the *Demandes d'Amour* and

[19] See my article, 'Un *Art d'Amour* inédit ...'

[20] A similar uncorrected error of copying occurs in the *Demandes d'Amour*, prose question 84 (see note 49 below).

the *De Amore*, when the two interlocutors put a couple of questions to each other at the close of Dialogue H.[21]

Whatever their precise origin, *Demandes d'Amour* assumed an identity of their own and survive rather as a single, loosely-connected text in variant form in a handful of manuscripts of the fourteenth and fifteenth centuries, as well as in some early printed works of the fifteenth and sixteenth centuries (see Appendix). Particular interest was shown in the *Demandes d'Amour* in the early years of this century, notably by Ernest Hoepffner, Alexander Klein (who edited, albeit poorly, the text of MS 16 F II), Walther Suchier, and Eero Ilvonen, with an examination of the various manuscripts containing the *Demandes* (especially Klein and Suchier), of the relationship between the *Demandes* and certain forms of the lyric, and more generally of the reflection in the *Demandes* of a continuing, aristocratic social pastime.[22] In a society so preoccupied with issues of love, from the earliest troubadours to the end of the Middle Ages and beyond, it is safe to assume that alongside the attested literary output on the subject there was much informal discussion; but beyond this there is some evidence of more systematic and organized discussion as a social game. The earliest hint of this occurs in Guillaume IX:

> Ieu conosc ben sen e folhor,
> E conosc anta e honor,
> E ai ardimen e paor;
> E si·m partetz un juec d'amor
> No suy tan fatz
> No·n sapcha triar lo melhor
> D'entre·ls malvatz.[23]

[21] Walsh, I, 6, Dialogue H, §§533–64 (pp. 199–209).

[22] Ernest Hoepffner, 'Frage- und Antwortspiele in der französischen Literatur des 14. Jahrhunderts', *Zeitschrift für romanische Philologie*, 33 (1909), 695–710; Alexander Klein, *Die altfranzösischen Minnefragen*, Marburger Beiträge zur romanischen Philologie, hg. von Ed. Wechssler, Heft I (Marburg: Adolf Ebel, 1911); Walther Suchier, 'Zu den altfranzösischen Minnefragen', *Zeitschrift für romanische Philologie*, 36 (1912), 221–28; Eero Ilvonen, 'Les demandes d'amour dans la littérature française du moyen âge', *Neuphilologische Mitteilungen*, 14 (1912), 128–44 (see also his review of Klein, ibid., 217–20). Klein's edition of MS 16 F II contains numerous errors of transcription: for instance, in the first prose question, he prints 'pour quoi' for 'pour quoy', 'parfaite' for 'parfaicte', 'seüt' for 'scet', and 'aurousé' for 'arrousé'. More serious are misreadings such as the following from prose question 41: 'fut et est (et) sempardurablement' for 'fut et est et sera pardurablement'.

[23] Quoted by Ilvonen, p. 128.

In its implied formality the allusion is not unlike the *disputatio* in which Jean de Meun later imagines Esperance engaged and hoping that her adherents in love would have 'le meilleur de la querele'.[24] If such socially organized debates on matters of love existed, they may merely have entailed putting two sides of a problem, or expressed opposing attitudes or alternative solutions, but they are likely to have led to a third party (individual or group) being asked to give a judgment or express an authoritative opinion. A thirteenth-century poem entitled *Ensenhamen de la donzela* by Amanieu de Sescas alludes to this possibility:

> si apelatz ab vos
> dels autres companhos
> que·us jutgen dreg o tort
> de vostre desacort.[25]

In Northern France there are sporadic allusions to a game known as 'le roi qui ne ment', and to 'le jeu du roi et de la reine'.[26] Reference to both of these games occurs in a late thirteenth-century poem, *Tournois de Chauvenci*, by Jacques Bretel:

> de ça karolent, et cil dancent;
> li vrai amant d'amors demandent,
> et li autres en determine
> le gieu del Roi, de la Roïne,
> et est fait par commandement;
> li tiers geue au Roi qui ne ment.[27]

Two texts from the early fourteenth century give us some clue to the procedure followed for 'le roi qui ne ment'. In Jean de Condé's *Sentier*

[24] *Roman de la Rose*, v. 4060. For further discussion of this moment in the *Rose*, see my article 'The continuator's monologue: Godefroy de Lagny and Jean de Meun', *French Studies*, 45 (1991), 1–16 (p. 11).

[25] Quoted by Ilvonen, p. 129.

[26] See E. Langlois, 'Le Jeu du Roi qui ne ment et le jeu du Roi et de la Reine', *Romanische Forschungen*, 23 (1907), 163–73. For a more recent investigation, see Richard Firth Green, 'Le Roi Qui ne ment and Aristocratic Courtship', in *Courtly Literature: Culture and Context*, Utrecht Publications in General and Comparative Literature, 25, edited by Keith Busby and Erik Kooper (Amsterdam–Philadelphia: John Benjamins, 1990), pp. 211–25.

[27] Quoted by Ilvonen, p. 136.

battu a group of ladies are playing the game; they elect a 'queen', who puts a question to each participant, and then receives questions in turn from them. In the *Voeux du Paon* by Jacques de Longuyon the arrangements are not quite the same: the five players first elect a 'king' from among their number, who then resolves the questions put by the other four.[28] Thus the game can take different forms, though E. Langlois has suggested that the game was originally called 'au Roi cui ne ment', with 'ment' as an imperative, so that the questions were about one's personal experience.[29] This suggested form of the game seems to be borne out by a reference in the *Chevalier de la Tour Landry* (late fourteenth century) in which knights and ladies 'jouoient au Roy qui ne ment pour dire verité du nom de s'amie'.[30] A more familiar, albeit confusing, allusion is to be found in the late thirteenth-century drama, the *Jeu de Robin et Marion*, when Huars, a peasant friend of Robin, suggests they collectively play 'as Roys et as Roïnes' (v. 442),[31] and a little later in the text Robin's cousin Baudons suggests the following:

> Je voeil, o Gautier Le Testu,
> Jüer as Rois et as Roïnes;
> Et je ferai demandes fines
> Se vous me volés faire roi (vv. 495–498).

Langlois explains that in attempting to ape an aristocratic pastime, the peasants have comically confused two separate games: they were really

[28] Details concerning these two texts have been taken from Ilvonen, p. 136, and Langlois, pp. 164–68. For an analysis of the questions posed in the *Voeux du Paon*, see E. Hoepffner, 'Les "Voeux du Paon" et les "Demandes amoureuses"', *Archivum Romanicum*, 4 (1920), 99–104. The four questions (and answers) correspond to prose questions 18, 19, 17, and 26 in MS 16 F II. As the *Voeux du Paon* is an early fourteenth-century text, Hoepffner concludes that collections of 'demandes d'amour' must already have existed by the very beginning of the fourteenth century, or even at the end of the thirteenth, and that the author of the *Voeux du Paon* drew on them and inserted them into his text (p. 104).

[29] Langlois, p. 163.

[30] Quoted by Langlois, p. 168.

[31] Quotations are taken from Adam le Bossu, *Le Jeu de Robin et Marion*, édité par E. Langlois, *CFMA* (Paris: Champion, 1924).

intending to play 'au roi qui ne ment'; 'le jeu du roi et de la reine' (singular, not plural) was actually a card game.[32]

That there is a link between the social game of 'le roi qui ne ment' and the *Demandes d'Amour* is clearly to be seen by the formulation of Prose question 82 (P.82)[33] in the text of MS 16 F II: 'Dame, je vous requier et prye moult amyablement par la force du jeu et par la foy que vous devez au roy qui ne ment, que vous me vueillez dire [...]'. Similarly in P.52 we find: 'Dame, je vous demande et prye par la force du jeu et du royaulme ou nul ne nulle ne doit mentir [...]'; and again in P.44 a further reference to the game which lies behind the *Demandes*: 'Beau Sire, je vous demande et pry par la force du jeu que [...]'. Are these direct reflections of questions used in an actual game, and are the questions and answers to be known by heart? Or are these questions merely in imitation of an actual game? At the same time and within the literary ambit of the later Middle Ages, these and other *Demandes*, consisting of an exchange between two interlocutors, have some affinity with the *débat*, which flourished particularly in the fourteenth and fifteenth centuries, with examples to be found among the works of Guillaume de Machaut, Froissart, Christine de Pisan, and especially Alain Chartier. Sometimes, but not always, their *débats* led to judgment, or to referral of the problem to a distinguished or appropriate person to judge, as in Alain Chartier's *Débat des Deux Fortunés d'Amours* and his *Livre des Quatre Dames*, or in Christine de Pisan's *Débat des Deux*

[32] Langlois, pp. 169–71. See also his note to v. 496 in his edition of *Le Jeu de Robin et Marion* (p. 66). Further references to the game of 'le roi qui ne ment' are to be found in Jean Froissart, *Le Joli Buisson de Jonece*, édité par Anthime Fourrier, *TLF* (Geneva: Droz, 1975), vv. 4427–28; Guillaume de Machaut, *Remede de Fortune*, vv. 767–70, in *Oeuvres de Guillaume de Machaut*, publiées par E. Hoepffner, *SATF*, 3 vols (Paris: Firmin Didot, 1908–21), II (1911), p. 28; and in his *Livre du Voir-Dit*, publié par Paulin Paris, Société des Bibliophiles français (Paris, 1875), v. 4979. In this text the poet, in his dream, leaves his mistress at one point in a melancholy mood, and happens upon a group of courtiers playing at 'le roi qui ne ment'; he asks a long question of the 'king' (vv. 2990–5243), receives a long reply (vv. 5254–5461), after which the company laughs; amid this excitement the dog barks loudly and wakes the dreamer! This light-hearted, comic tone underlines the fact that it was a game.

[33] Throughout the analysis of the *Demandes d'Amour* the verse questions will be referred to as V.1, V.2, etc., and those in prose as P.1, P.2, etc.

Amans,[34] while two of Machaut's poems are entitled *Jugement dou Roy de Behaigne* and *Jugement dou Roi de Navarre*,[35] thus putting the emphasis on the judgment after lengthy debate. To give a judgment is close to giving an answer as in the *Demandes*, and the text which offers the most extensive and authoritative of such judgments is perhaps Martial d'Auvergne's *Arrêts d'Amour*, a mid-fifteenth century text consisting of fifty-one judgments delivered by a court of love.[36] More immediately related to the *Demandes d'Amour*, though, is a text such as Eustache Deschamps's *Plusieurs demandes entre les dames avecques les responses sur ce*, containing thirty-five questions and answers,[37] while Christine de Pisan refers directly to the social practice in her *Dit de la Rose*:

La n'ot parlé a ce mangier
Fors de courtoisie et d'onnour ...
Et de beaulx livres et de dis,
Et de balades plus de dix,
Qui mieulx mieulx chascun devisoit,
Ou d'amours qui s'en avisoit
Ou de demandes gracieuses.[38]

Between discussion, debate, judgment, and question and answer there is an obvious link, and the formulation of debates and questions and answers clearly owes much to scholastic training, as is attested in such poems as the *Altercatio Phyllidis et Florae* and other similar texts often referred to under the heading of *débats du clerc et du chevalier*.[39] Like-

[34] *The Poetical Works of Alain Chartier*, edited by J. C. Laidlaw (Cambridge University Press, 1974), pp. 155–304, and Introduction, pp. 29–36; and *Oeuvres poétiques de Christine de Pisan*, publiées par Maurice Roy, *SATF*, 3 vols. (Paris: Firmin Didot, 1886–96), II (1891), pp. 49–109.

[35] Machaut, *Oeuvres*, I.57–135 and 137–282.

[36] *Les Arrêts d'Amour de Martial d'Auvergne*, publiées par Jean Rychner, *SATF* (Paris: Picard, 1951).

[37] *Oeuvres complètes d'Eustache Deschamps*, publiées par le Marquis de Queux de Saint-Hilaire et Gaston Raynaud, *SATF*, 11 vols. (Paris: Firmin Didot, 1878–1903), VIII (1893), pp. 112–125. See also Klein, pp. 263–78.

[38] *Oeuvres poétiques*, II.31 (vv. 68–75).

[39] See Charles Oulmont, *Les débats du clerc et du chevalier dans la littérature poétique du moyen âge* (Paris: Champion, 1911) and Giuseppe Tavani, 'Il dibattito sul chierico e il cavaliere nella tradizione mediolatina e volgare', *Romanistisches Jahrbuch*, 15 (1964), 51–84. A version of the *Altercatio* is also to be found in A. Bömer, 'Das Vagantenlied von Phyllis und Flora, nach einer Niederschrift des ausgehenden 12. Jahrhunderts', *Zeitschrift für deutsches Altertum*, 56 (1918), 217–39.

wise a scholastic background will be evident in the *Demandes d'Amour*.

In the collection contained in Royal MS 16 F II there are eighteen verse questions followed by eighty-eight in prose, and once again it seems as though this particular collection is an amalgam of two traditions, one of questions in verse, the other of questions in prose. According to Ilvonen,[40] the designation *demandes d'amour* refers primarily to prose questions, though clearly the scribe of MS 16 F II intended the title to embrace the questions and answers in both prose and verse. Most manuscripts of the *Demandes* contain either verse or prose questions; only two of those described and published by Klein have both, 16 F II and Westminster Abbey MS 21, though the two manuscripts which he did not edit, Chantilly, Musée Condé 654 and Wolfenbüttel, Herzog August 84.7.Aug.2, also contain both (see Appendix). It is clear even from the incomplete account of collections that Klein published that occasionally a verse question can become a prose one, or vice-versa (see Appendix), while any clear distinction between verse and prose questions is further blurred in the series of *demandes d'amour* inserted as a social game in a late fourteenth-century text, the *Chevalier Errant* of Thomas of Saluzzo.[41] They are written basically in prose, but in such a way as to 'lasciar manifestamente apparire le rime tra la prosa'.[42] Collectively they show that the questions and answers had achieved some degree of fixity, though they do not appear in the same order from one manuscript to another among those manuscripts which contain the verse questions.[43] Some of the questions in the *Chevalier Errant* are word for word the same as the verse questions in MS 16 F II, but they are interspersed with other questions that have no clear equivalent in either the verse or prose questions of the Royal MS, and they

[40] Ilvonen, p. 129.

[41] Anna Maria Finoli, 'Un gioco di società, "Le roi qui ne ment", e le "demandes en amour" nel "Chevalier errant" di Tommaso III di Saluzzo', *Studi Francesi*, 27 (1983), 257–64.

[42] Finoli, p. 259.

[43] The MSS which Klein lists as containing the verse questions, apart from Royal 16 F II, are: B.N. fr. 12615, Cheltenham, Phillipps 8336 (now British Library, Additional 46919), Montpellier, Fac. Méd. 236, Arsenal 5203, and the Westminster Abbey 'Poésies françaises' (MS 21). Chantilly, Musée Condé 654 and Wolfenbüttel, Herzog August, 84.7.Aug.2 also contain verse questions. For a comparative table indicating the appearance of the verse questions in these MSS see Appendix, and Klein, pp. 26–27.

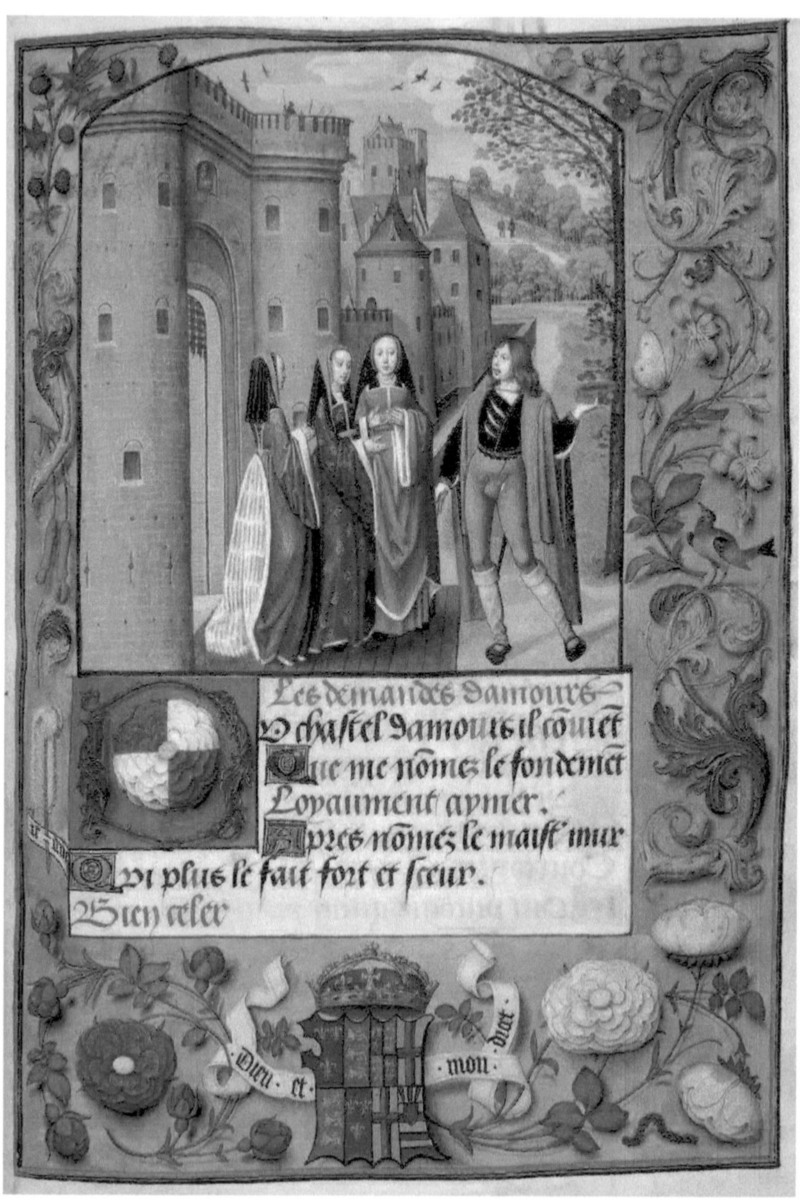

Plate 2: 'The *chastel d'amours*' (Royal MS 16 F II, f° 188r). Reproduced by permission of the British Library.

are found in the following order: V.15, V.16, V.17, [...], V.18, [...], V.10, V.11, V.13, V.14, V.8, V.9, V.1, V.2, V.3, V.4, V.5, V.6, V.7, [...].[44]

In some of the manuscripts in which the verse questions occur they are given the title 'Chastel d'Amours'.[45] It is easy to see that such a title would be appropriate for the first seven verse questions in MS 16 F II. Indeed the illustration (see Plate 2) and text on f. 188r effect a fusion of the traditions of the *demandes d'amour* and *chastel d'amour*, in that the text is headed 'Les Demandes d'Amour', while the illustration shows a young man talking with a group of noble ladies who are standing outside a castle, clearly the *chastel d'amour*, of which, symbolically, the portcullis is up and the entrance open.[46] This may well be less a question of deliberate fusion than of illustrating the image with which the verse questions open. Of the title 'Chastel d'Amours' Ilvonen writes: 'L'amour courtois y est comparé à une forteresse, avec ses *fondemens*, *crenels*, *gardes*, etc. Le but du poème est de renseigner le *loyal amant* sur les moyens de s'emparer des clefs de cette forteresse, et de pénétrer jusqu'aux salles et aux manoirs où la joie parfaite l'attend'.[47] The general imagery of these first seven questions owes something to the *Roman de la Rose*, and they form a tightly-knit, logical sequence, like succeeding stanzas of a poem. It is as though we are building the castle from stanza to stanza, from the foundations to the inner chambers, a process not unlike that used by Christine de Pisan in her *Livre de la Cité des Dames*; while the answers are presented as semi-allegorical figures, e.g. V.2:

> Aprés nommez le maistre mur,
> Qui plus le fait fort et sceür?
> Bien celer.

After V.7 the castle image is lost and the questions become more general and more loosely connected. The next six follow the same structural pattern as the first seven, with two rhyming octosyllabics forming the

[44] See note 33 above.

[45] See Hoepffner, 'Frage- und Antwortspiele ...', p. 703. The MSS which bear this title are British Library, Additional 46919 (formerly Cheltenham, Phillipps 8336) ('Veyes cy le chastel de leal amour', Klein, p. 147) and Arsenal 5203 (a copy of Berne 218) ('Ci commence le chastel d'Amours', Klein, p. 153).

[46] The colours in this illustration are as rich and varied as those on f. 137r described in note 10 above.

[47] Ilvonen, pp. 137–38.

question, followed by a non-rhyming half-line or shorter line for the answer (V.7, which appears to be an exception, was probably intended to have a two-line answer of five syllables each, rather than one long decasyllabic line). The use of allegory also persists for a while, the questions in both V.8 and V.9 being introduced by 'Qui fait [...]?', together with answers 'Bien parler' and 'Courtoysie'. V.14 introduces a variation in the structural pattern, with a four-line question in rhyming couplets, and a momentary change of perspective, too, in that this question, unlike the first thirteen, is for the benefit of the lady, rather than for the male lover, though at the same time he would understand from the question why he is being refused. For the final four questions, however, he becomes once more the beneficiary of the questions, which are spread respectively over two, three, four, and four lines, containing rhyming couplets, apart from V.16, which has three lines on the same rhyme.

None of these questions is unique to MS 16 F II, nor is this series of eighteen the most extensive: Paris, Bibliothèque Nationale MS français 12615 has twenty-nine of them.[48] In general the verse questions and answers read rather like a riddle, which accounts in part for the degree of similarity in the wording of comparable questions from manuscript to manuscript. The concepts of rhythm and rhyme often seem poor, and the formulation of the questions is at times somewhat convoluted.

What, overall, would the intended reader learn from these verse questions and answers? The first six would teach him that the way to conquest is through loving loyally and secretly, by looking (lovingly) but exercising restraint, and by declaring one's love wisely; he is to recognise an encouraging response, and is ensured of surpassing delight; the 'castle' is then maintained by living joyously and dressing elegantly, in other words, by being a socially pleasant person (V.7). He learns too (V.8–13) that the pleasure of fair speech can win fair lady, and that love is sustained by the exercise of 'courtoysie', in which secrecy is an important element, a sweet kiss or a glance a prized favour, but a rebuff no laughing matter; on the other hand, that it is by refusal that a lady can test her beseeching lover (V.14); finally (V.15–18), that love is nurtured in hope, that fair speech, though of great value, may desert him in the event, that pretence, though the villainous aspect of love, is to be embraced (shades of Jean de Meun), and that the most visible outward sign of love is to blush or grow pale ('muer couleur').

[48] See Klein, pp. 143–47.

The eighty-eight prose questions which follow on from the verse questions represent by far the largest collection among the manuscripts that Klein published, though the unpublished Chantilly MS has over twice as many.[49] Even so nine of them (P.15, P.21, P.44, P.48, P.49, P.61, P.65, P.68, and P.78) appear to be unique to MS 16 F II (see Appendix). The prose questions consist of an exchange between a lady and gentleman, who address each other formally as 'Beau Sire' and 'Dame'. Fifty-two of the questions are addressed by the lady to the man (P.1–51 and P.62), thirty-six by the man to the lady (P.52–61 and P.63–88). The length and complexity of the questions or answers vary, but most consist merely of one question followed by the answer. Some, however, do have a secondary exchange, when the person putting the original question requests an expansion of the answer given, as for example in P.38, when the lady asks for an explanation of the 'quatre desirs' mentioned in the answer she had received. A total of nineteen answers prompt a supplementary question of some kind.[50] In P.68 the reason for the supplementary question is that the first answer is not a full reply to the question put, while in P.44 the second question really builds on the answer to the first and puts a separate question leading on from the first. Klein, in fact, treats these as two separate questions and answers,[51] which is why he attributes a total of eighty-nine prose questions to MS 16 F II. In all other instances the supplementary question is merely formulaic: twelve have 'Raison pourquoy?' (P.51, P.55, P.56, P.57, P.58, P.59, P.61, P.69, P.70, P.79, P.80, and P.81), two have 'Cause pourquoy?' (P.63 and P.65), one has 'Sire, pourquoy?' (P.1), and one 'Dame, pourquoy?' (P.83).

Although statements or advice are sometimes attributed to 'la rigle d'amours' or to 'l'amant' in the exchanges between 'l'amant' and 'l'amante' in the *Art d'Amour*, the overwhelming impression in that text is that wisdom and knowledge are dispensed primarily by women – Heloise, and 'la dame qui le maisgre cheval chevaulchoit'. The division of the questions and answers in the *Demandes d'Amour* between the lady and gentleman helps to impart a clear and differentiating identity in this regard to each

[49] The most that any of the other MSS published by Klein has is forty-six.

[50] P.84, in which the answer to P.83 has been repeated by the scribe in error from P.83, has not been included in this count.

[51] Klein, p. 50. The scribe, who marks clearly the beginning of each question with an illuminated gold capital, treats P.44 as one question with a supplementary, not as two separate items.

of the two treatises. No intended reader of the *Demandes d'Amour* is seriously going to concern himself with whether technically it is the man or the lady who asks more questions; the overall impression is that each needs guidance and reassurance from the other in matters of love. Thus there is a stylised dialogue, in which each draws on the other's wisdom, experience, or insight, for although a few of the questions could equally have been asked by the other person and the same response received (e.g., P.42, P.48, P.80, or P.85), most questions are either specifically worded in a way which is appropriate for the person to whom they are put (e.g., P.24, P.25, P.28, P.34, or P.37 addressed to the man, and P.52, P.53, P.57, P.58, or P.60 addressed to the lady), or in the case of questions which could have been put to either, the answer seems to accord with the outlook of the person giving it (e.g., P.27, P.29, or P.30 for the man answering, and P.61, P.62, or P.70 for the lady answering). This appropriateness of the questions or answers should not, however, be stressed too much, for there is no hint of any rigid divide, hostility, or confrontation; rather the treatise is enriched by the underlying assumption that love is a sympathetically shared experience. Even in those instances in which the question is clearly framed with the other person's experience in mind, the very fact of asking the question displays an awareness by the questioner of the particular situation or problem that could arise for the other person. The tone, then, is never misogynistic or satirical, and the bawdiness of some collections finds no place in MS 16 F II.[52] The answers are always correct, in the widest sense, while the essential formalism gives the impression at times that the questions and answers are less informational than catechismal (e.g. P.17).

The type of question asked varies. The simplest, though not necessarily the easiest to answer, merely asks for a definition: what is love? (P.30); honour? (P.85); generosity? (P.86); courtesy? (P.87). Other questions seek an explanation: why does love not make the detractors themselves love, to stop them being envious of lovers? (P.21); why is jealousy unavoidable? (P.49); what is the cause of sighing in love? (P.67). In the overwhelming majority of questions, however, the respondent is presented with a choice: on love in general, for example, the man is asked which is better, love long desired or love easily attained? (P.14); followed by which love is the more secure, that which is lightly given, or that which is long desired? (P.15).

[52] See Firth Green, p. 221.

Sometimes choice is only implied, by requiring an answer 'yes' or 'no': does love end? (P.41); should a lover be jealous of his or her loved one? (P.48); can a woman have two lovers? (P.71). In such questions, as in all those which involve choice, the answer is always justified or explained, either spontaneously (often by the use of 'car') or in response to a supplementary question as indicated above. Most memorable, perhaps, are those questions which describe in some detail hypothetical situations for which a choice is asked, or pose specific problems requiring a recommendation: if another man loved your mistress, would you prefer to meet him as you went in to see her and he was coming out, or vice versa? (P.24); would you prefer your mistress to be attractive but not very clever, or clever but not very attractive? (P.37); if a man loves a woman, but can get no welcoming response from her, only persistent refusal and discouragement, and another woman approaches him telling him that he is wasting his time with his loved one and tenderly offering him her love in turn, should he abandon the love which looks hopeless and respond to the love offered by the second woman? (Answer: no) (P.59). Some of these seem unintentionally comic in their seriousness: if a damsel, courted by two men, borrows a horse from one and boots and a hat from the other in order to go on a journey, which one does she love best? (P.58); when three men all love the same woman, and they go to her and ask her to choose between them, so she squeezes the finger of one, stamps on the toe of the second, and casts glances at the third, which does she love best? (P.64).

The answers to these two questions, as to others, may appear banal and obvious, yet many of the questions display a considerable degree of scholastic subtlety: is there more of you in love, or love in you? (P.2); is there more good than ill in love? (P.3); would you prefer that a loyal and trusted friend should marry your mistress, or you his? (P.12); which is better in love, wisdom or concealment? (P.31); which is better in love, wisdom or loyalty? (P.32); while the answer to the question 'what is love?' is that it is an invisible force, whose substance and works indicate one's disposition and manner of loving, and that it starts by the sight of the beloved (P.30). The generalities inherent in such questions are also to be found in questions concerning gender differences: who is more tormented by love, men or women? (P.61); whose love lasts longer, that of a man, or that of a woman? (P.62); who sighs more deeply for love, a man or a woman? (P.69).

When the prose questions are read through, the order in which they occur appears somewhat arbitrary, but they are not completely disjointed, as one often leads on to another, e.g., P.16–17, P.18–19, P.20–24, P.27–30, P.31–32, P.33–37, P.38–39, P.41–42, P.43–45, P.67–69, or P.74–75, while P.46–55 form a sequence on aspects of jealousy. The variety, range and general mix of questions account in part for the overall impression of formlessness. With regard to variety and range, Richard Firth Green divides the kind of questions asked in collections of *Demandes d'Amour* in general into three types: those on the code of love, those which involve specific problems, and those which place the respondent in a hypothetical situation.[53] These categories could equally be applied to the prose questions in MS 16 F II, but another way of dividing them would be to make two broad groups, one containing questions of a purely objective nature, the other questions requiring some personal response. In this way the objective questions would far outnumber the others, but the basis of such a division would be to some extent undermined by the fact that in order to reply to the objective questions the respondent would have to draw on the experience of being or having been in love. Likewise personal experience is implicit in the questions asked. Nevertheless, if one were to leave aside all those questions which deal with hypothetical situations or require a specifically personal response, and redefine Firth Green's first category ('code of love') as 'general questions requiring objective answers on the code of love, its definition, nature, or effects on lovers', it would again be found that questions can run in sequences: P.3–4, P.13–19, P.21–23, P.27–36, P.38–44, P.46–50, P.52–55, P.60–62, P.67–71, P.73–75, and P.81–88 (a total of fifty-seven questions).

A closer examination of the answers to the questions will provide a clearer impression of the instruction given and the attitudes being recommended to the reader. Overall the picture is a conventional one. Love, described in P.30 (see above), is commonly inspired by beauty (P.33–34), but that inspired by character (good sense, wisdom, or intelligence) will be the longer lasting (P.36); it is therefore better to have a mistress who is clever (wise?) but only moderately attractive, than one who is attractive but not very clever (wise) (P.37). Beauty, in any case, is relative and in the eye of the beholder (P.78). Love comes from God, Who is love (P.42); it has no end (P.41), and was established to bestow joy, for the promotion of all good things, to inspire honour, to provide a discipline, and for the sake of procreation (P.40). Loyalty in love is of prime importance, so that

[53] Firth Green, p. 215.

the refusal or indifference of a loved one should not be a reason for abandoning that love in favour of love offered by another (P.20, P.59, P.63, P.76 and P.77). The way to obtain the grace of a woman's love is by being courteous, loyal, resolute, honest, secretive, unpretentious, moderate and discreet (P.74, P.75 and P.82). Women also admire prowess and boldness, as it enhances their reputations to be loved by someone with such characteristics (P.83). The virtues of courtliness, generosity, and a sense of honour are extolled (P.85–87), while a woman's good reputation should always be upheld, even if it belies one's own experience of her (P.6). Desire and anticipation or a promise are sweeter than fulfilment (P.1, P.7–8, P.14, and P.25), and hope is a great gift of love (P.3–4, P.18). Moreover a long-awaited love is more secure when it is eventually bestowed than one which is easily won (P.15). On the other hand it can require more skill to preserve a love than to attain it in the first place (P.16).

Love imparts more good than sorrow (P.3). As for the detractors ('mesdisans'), they should not be a reason for abandoning love (P.20). Their evil, moreover, can be turned to account, since it makes a lover appreciate the good things (P.21) and become wiser and more self-controlled (P.22); but because of the risk of what others may say in order to destroy a good relationship, it is better to see a rival leaving as you are going to see your beloved than that you should be leaving when he arrives, for this gives you the opportunity of putting right any bad impression he may have created (P.24). A lover therefore feels insecure, even when love seems assured, and this can lead to jealousy (P.46).

Jealousy is born of suspicion (P.47). It is difficult to avoid it, partly because hearts tend to waver (P.48–49). Women can be as jealous as men (P.52), and their jealousy can be more intense (P.55), while a man's jealousy may be more persistent (P.54). A woman's jealousy is justified by a man's tendency to inconstancy, which comes about because of his greater freedom of movement (P.53). Jealousy can be both a good and a bad thing: it inspires to greater efforts, but it is bad in that it causes a lover to doubt the goodness of the person loved (P.50). The feeling of insecurity is reflected in the recommendation never to reveal the name of the person of whom one is jealous, lest one's mistress be thus encouraged to think of that person once he has been named! (P.51). A note of calculation and self-interest is also found in the recommendation that it is better to take your friend's loved one to wife than that he should take yours, as you could then have the best of both worlds! (P.12).

Women suffer more than men for love, because they cannot declare their feelings openly (P.61 and P.69). They have to conceal their desires more than men for the sake of their honour (P.70); their love tends to be longer lasting (P.62); they must be careful with giving and receiving gifts (P.81). A woman cannot divide her heart between two lovers (P.71).

* * *

Despite differences of approach and scope between the two love-treatises preserved in MS 16 F II, the view of love being offered to the young Prince Arthur is essentially uniform in its seriousness and high-mindedness, and totally dependent upon tradition. These are positive qualities, entirely appropriate for their purpose. The novice of the *Art d'Amour*, learning precepts and the way to petition for his love and attain his desire, is to some extent reflected in the verse section of the *Demandes d'Amour*, while in the prose questions the reader is witness to an exchange of distilled wisdom between experienced adults. The *Demandes d'Amour* thus reinforce the fundamental attitudes and tenets of the *Art d'Amour*, so that throughout a broadly similar image of love is projected: its essential nobility, the unavoidability of suffering, its inspirational value, the need to persevere to obtain a promised reward, the need to behave honourably and to be worthy of love, the importance of sight as the mainspring of love, the difficulties of maintaining love, the need for restraint, the problems of detractors and the importance of preserving a woman's reputation. While these are some of the aspects shared by both texts, the *Art d'Amour* has dimensions unknown to the *Demandes*: the social differences (apart from P.72), compatibility, judgment, recompense and punishment, and aspects of behaviour such as the avoidance of gossip, care over promises, flattery, over-indulgence, or foolishness. The muddled state of Heloise's *Art d'Amour* cannot totally erase its undoubted qualities, though the collection of *Demandes d'Amour* certainly makes for easier reading, in spite of a few obscurities (e.g., V.6 or P.10). Intermingled with the more abstract questions and answers, the hypothetical situations remain in the mind as examples, promoting attitudes and reactions that could be applied to other similar circumstances. It is one of the cruel ironies of history that the wealth of human experience reflected in the poems and treatises of Royal MS 16 F II should have been available to its intended recipient for so short a time.

The text

The text of the *Art d'Amour* and of the *Demandes d'Amour* has been edited on the whole conservatively, with changes made only in the interest of comprehension of the text or of grammatical accuracy (e.g., agreements, verb-endings), and with sparing use of accents. Rejected readings are signalled in the text by the use of asterisks, and are placed at the foot of the page. Deletion of letters or words is indicated by round brackets, insertion by square brackets.

HELOISE'S *ART D'AMOUR*

137r Tous ceulx qui ce livre veullent entendre doivent savoir que,
quant maistre Pierre Abaielart eut longuement regné et usé de ses
137v arts, sa conscience le reprist. Il fonda une abbaye pres / de Sayne,
en la terre de Champaigne, que l'en appelle l'abbaye du Paraclit. En
celle abbaye du Paraclit fut une nonain esleue abbesse, laquelle eut
nom Heloys. Icelle Heloys fut bien introduite en la science des sept
arts, et selon l'estat des sept arts elle eut sept graces: c'est assavoir,
mauvaises parolles eschiever, mauvaises ouyes fuyr, mauvais
voyemens, mauvais contenemens, vivre sans rapine et sans mauvais
attouchemens; sur toutes riens elle hayoit luxure. Et pour ce toutes
gens qui veulent estre esprouvez en l'art d'Amours et la garder et
maintenir doyvent louer l'abbesse Heloys, qui enseigne ung sien
disciple, qui Gaultier ot nom.[1]

Premierement elle lui demonstre, se il la veult croire, comment
il se pourra maintenir et gouverner entre les vrays amans, et soy
bien garder, sans estre blecié des darts d'Amours. Ainsi pourra estre
138r le disciple vray amant nouvel / chevallier, fuyre la sayette qui les
aucuns navre et occist, chevallier pourra estre et les commandemens
d'Amours garder.[2]

Le premier commandement d'Amour si vient de l'ueil.[3] Et couvient que de l'ueil le commandement d'Amour touche au cuer de l'amant. Amour est premierement dicte d'amer [se] l'entablement d'amour congnoist les cuers des deux gens amans. Amour a tel droit en soy qu'elle est acquise par continuee retenue, amenuysee et crevee par fuyr. Qui veult amour vrayement demener, vrayement doit amer, et foy doit tenir et garder, et loyaulté avoir en soy.

Premierement nous devons savoir que amour est passion de
souffrir; car ainçois que amour soit vrayement parfaicte, il couvient
qu'elle soit pesee en droit poiz des cuers des deux amans. Nu(u)lle
chose n'est plus griefve que vraye amour maintenir; car le vray
138v amant doubte / tousjours que l'entablement d'amours ne faille.
Tous amans doubtent tousjours qu'ilz ne mettent leurs labeurs en
vaynes euvres. Les amans craingnent et doubtent que mauvaises

Notes will be found at the end of the texts, starting on p. 93.

parolles ne leur nuysent. Les amans doubtent que aucuns par dons et par promesses ne soubztrayent leurs amours. Se les amans sont povres, ilz doubtent tousjours que celles qu'ilz ayment ne les despisent pour leur povreté, et que leur amour sy ne soit corrumpue par defaulte de donner. Se les personnes amans sont riches et puissans d'avoir, tousjours donnent et prennent, car ilz se doubtent que s'ilz failloyent a prendre et a donner, que leur amour defaudroit.

Nul ne peut vrayement raconter toutes les paours des amans,
donques passion d'amour est dicte quant de chascune des deux partyes
139r amour est droictement pesee. Meilleur chose est / aux amans qu'ilz
laissent leurs amours qu'ilz ont acquises sans riens donner, que ilz
perdent leurs amours gaingnees et conquises par dons. Tous amans
doubtent que mesdisans ne leur troublent et empeschent leurs
amours.

L'abbesse Heloys monstre a son disciple par certaines raisons comment povres amans ne se peuent si bien ordonner a servir Amours comme les nobles et les riches; car les povres amans n'ont dont ilz puissent nourrir droicturierement leurs amours.

L'en doit savoir que toute femme qui est armee de trop grant diversité de couleur, tout amant doibt fuir, et parellement doit la femme l'omme. L'en doit savoir que l'en ne doit pas surfaire la beaulté de la femme, mais les bonnes meurs.

L'abbesse Heloys demonstre et si enseigne a son disciple qu'il
139v garde que le malice de folle femme ne le deçoive, / car la nature de
fole femme est telle, et a les parolles si plaines de grant doulceur que
puis que la femme a l'omme enlacié, a paine se peut puis deslacier
de ses las.

La proesse des bonnes meurs acquiert amour vraye, et lui donne
le resplendissement de vrayement amer. Se les corps sont sages et ne
sont pas beaulx, s'ilz sont plains de bonnes meurs, Amours lors les
doit recevoir. Les amans qui sont sages ne se peulent point desvoyer
de l'accord d'amours, ne ne sont pas de leger meüz par aucune vaine
parolles. L'amant qui sage est a grant paine peut respondre ses
entalentemens ne desirs de la voix de sa sage amye. Se l'amant est
sage de la doctrine de lui, sa doctrine introduit la contenance de celle
qu'il ayme. Tout amant doit querre amye qui soit remplie de la rigle
de bonnes meurs. Amant ne doit pas querre lignage, beaulté, ne
140r richesse de celle qu'il veult amer, mais / tant seulement qu'elle soit
plaine de bonté. Bonté fait tout amant requerir en noblesse. Toutes

manieres de gens vindrent premierement d'Adam, nostre premier pere, mais nous n'avons pas tous une fourme ne une semblance en habondance de richesses ne contenement de corps. Amant ne doit requerre que planté de bonnes meurs. Noblesse si est differente entre toutes gens, mais l'en doit savoir que moult de manieres de gens est qui sont extraitz de noblesse et laissent l'estat et la voye dont ilz sont nez et se prennent et aherdent a rudesse. Et aucune fois avient que l'amant qui n'est pas né de noble lignaige a plus de grace et de proesse en soy que celui qui est (ex) extrait de noble lieu. Et par ceste raison seulle prouesse d'amour est digne de louenge.

L'abondance de bonnes parolles esmeuvent souvent les cuers des
140v amans plus a amer que a malice. Sou- / vent avient que l'ordannance de belles parolles et honnestes apelle et admonneste les cuers des amans a amer. La belle parolle fait souvent acquerre loz et proesse.

L'abbesse Heloys du Paraclit cy enseigne et demonstre a son disciple que aucune dame qui est nee du peuple, aucune si est plus noble et aucune si est mains noble. Aussi est il entre les hommes; l'un est du peuple et l'autre est noble.

Et aucunesfois avient que, quant l'amant veult parler a son amye, il pert sa contenance par le regard d'elle. Aucun amant si est qui par esbahissement de parler et deffault de contenance pert toute la force et la vigueur d'amour qu'il a conceue, et ne peut riens dire qui plaise. Et ainsi il est tenu pour fol et pour cognard. Il couvient que tous amans soyent saiges et garniz de hardiesse qui parler veulent a leurs amyes, autrement toute la flambe d'amour est amortie. /

141r Se l'amant est menacié ou escondit de s'amye, il se doit departir d'elle courtoisement celle fois, sans trop parler et sans soy courroucier. Se il a temps et lieu de demourer, il doit parler d'aucunes belles parolles bien ordonnees, ou d'aucun conte ou d'aucune chose nouvelle qui esmeuve le cuer de s'amye a joye, et loer la personne d'elle; car femme est de telle nature qu'elle s'esjouyst de leger quant l'en la loue; femme croit de leger a tout ce que appartient a la louenge de soy. Par toutes ces choses l'amant peult parler a s'amye en soy gardant de la courroucier, et* c'est par ceste raison, car malice trop plus croist en la femelle que ou masle.

Et demonstre que depuis xiiii ans jusques a soixante homme peut porter les armes d'amours, et la femme de douze jusques a quarante.[4]

141v Et demonstre l'abbesse Heloys du Paraclit / que par cincq

*MS: courroucier tout homme qui a quatorse ans et

manieres amour si est acquise entre les vrais amans, c'est assavoir par noblesse, par beaulté, par prouesse, par embrasement de courtoisie, par ordonnance de belles parolles, par habondance de richesses, et par conception de regard.

L'abbesse Heloys demonstre et si enseigne que tous amans doivent avoir dixhuit ans avant qu'ilz puissent droitturie[re]ment prendre les armes d'amours, car a dixhuit ans pour petit de chose se repentiroyent pour la honte. Et pour ce amour est empeschee entre les amans jusques a xviii ans.

L'abbesse Heloys demonstre et si enseigne que devant la fin de son livre enseignera a son disciple pourquoy amours est plus ardant en l'amour du masle que de la femelle.[5] Et demonstre cy a son disciple que nul aveugle ne peut loyaulment amer, car par la veue est amour conceue.

142r L'abbesse Heloys demonstre a son disci- / ple que trop grant habondance de delit empesche a amer, car aucuns amans sont si plains de l'abondance de delit qu'ilz ne peulent entrer en la raiz d'amours.

Aucuns amans sont qui puis qu'ilz ont perdu la veue de ce qu'ilz aiment, ilz se departent de legier et se adonnent a autre amer; et telle nature si est de femme. Tous amans convoitent de legier ce qu'ilz voyent, et la maniere de telz amans est semblable au chien qui est en gest, et comparable aux asnes qui riens ne scevent. Et telle nature est de legier esmeue, mais raison humaine dessevre la nature d'omme et de femme de la nature des bestes mues.

L'abbesse Heloys demontre et enseigne que entre homme et femme amour est acquise en v. manieres, c'est assavoir par beauté, par promesse, par bonnes meurs, par belles parolles, par richesses, et par l'ottroyance de la chose requise. Et les trois premieres raisons
142v d'amours ac- / quierent les deux derrenieres. La delectableté de la beaulté par petit travail acquiert amour. Les petits amans ne requierent plus fors qu'ilz ayent ce qu'ilz couvoitent, et qu'ilz ayment la semblance, la fourme, et le contenement de ce qu'ilz desirent.

L'abbesse Heloys demonstre et aussi enseigne a son disciple que amour ne se peult longuement absconcer entre les sages amans; et dit que les acroissemens d'amours ostent de legier et amenuysent le sens des saiges amans. L'amour qui est publiee ne garde pas l'estat ne la rigle d'amour.

Il avient souvent que par la male renommee des mesdisans les

amans laissent a amer, et poise moult souvent aux amans qu'onques
se prindrent a amer. Et entre ces amans qui sont diffamez par parolles
de mesdisans amour ne peut durer. Souvent avient que telz amans
143r ne peulent retenir a eulx les soulas de leurs amours. / Et souvent
avient que les aucuns sont sages et se gardent par leur souspeçon
qu'ilz ont que mesdisans ne leur nuysent. Et de telle amour maintenir
souvent avient que les amans, par la doubtance d'iceulx mesdisans,
en cheent ou dangier de mort. Et en telle amour les amans se doubtent
et ne peuent avoir soulas de ce qu'ilz couvoitent. Et telz amans
s'eschauffent de plus en plus sans attemperance. Et aucune fois avient
que l'amour de telz amans vient au neant; car tous amans s'efforcent
a acomplir la chose qui leur est ottroyee.

Tous saiges amans doivent querre amyes qui soyent leur pareil,
et qui soyent plaines de bonnes meurs selon leur estat.

L'en doit savoir que toutes passions que povres amans seuffrent
viennent et naissent premierement de la pensee propre, qui est
conceue d'eulx mesmes par l'entablement des deux amans. L'abbesse
143v Heloys nous demonstre / que, quant une dame est couvenable a
porter les armes d'amours et est en sa franchise, les amans la
couvoitent tantost. L'amour des dames par seulle consideration de
pensees ardent et eschaufent de plus en plus jusques a ce qu'ilz
viennent a leurs desirs et a leurs voulentez. Adonques couvient aux
amans concevoir en leurs cuers les formes et beaultez des amantes,
leurs corps et leurs contenances, leurs fais et leurs ditz et leurs
manieres. Aprés que les amans ont toutes ces choses regardees et
conceues en leurs cuers, ilz ne peulent plus retenir leurs frainz contre
les dartz d'amours. Toutes ces choses dessus veu[e]s et conceues, les
amans si ne finent de penser comment ilz puissent venir a perfection
de leurs amours. Donc quierent les amans temps et ayde, comment
ils puissent avoir la grace de celles qu'ilz ayment. /

144r L'abbesse Heloys demonstre a son disciple que ceste passion
d'amour est armee de la pure pensee du regard des cuers des deux
amans; c'est assavoir que passion d'amour par droite nature et par
raison doit estre entre homme et femme, et non pas entre deux
hommes ne entre deux femmes, car les deux hommes sont d'une
nature et d'une matire et les femmes d'une autre. L'abbesse Heloys
si enseigne et demonstre que ce que nature donne,[6] toute amour fuit
– les contenances, les accointemens, les efforcemens, aussi les
contenemens. Les entablemens des vrais amans ne requierent qu'ilz

puissent perseverer en penser a acomplir leurs voulentez de ce qu'ilz ayment.

L'abbesse Heloys demonstre et enseigne que par dons et par promesses aucunesfois les amans qui sont en leurs franchises se soubzmettent a la jurisdiction d'aultruy. Ceste rigle se tient aux
144v povres amans, / car les povres amans deffaillent souvent a
l'acomplissement de leur desir par povreté. L'en apperçoit souvent, par prouvable argument, la ou les richesses faillent les amours amortissent entre les amans.

L'abbesse Heloys demonstre et enseigne a son disciple que amour si est dicte l'amaison ou les cueurs des amans sont prins par leurs regars ou par leurs contenances, et par penser a ceulx qu'ilz ayment. Nulle obscurté ne peut estaindre la lumiere des vrais amans.

L'abbesse Heloys demonstre et enseigne a son disciple que amour fait les couars hardis, les rudes courtois, les avaricieux moult larges, et les bas met en noblesse treshault.

L'abbesse Heloys demonstre et enseigne a son disciple quelle maniere de gent est couvenable a porter les armes d'amours. Elles sont portees par sens, par beaulté, par courtoisie, par prouesse, par
145r noblesse, par largesse, par loyaulté. Par sens il / couvient que les
amans soyent saiges a garder eulx et ce qu'ilz ayment. Par beaulté il couvient que les amans se tiennent nettement a celle fin qu'ilz plaisent a ce qu'ilz ayment. Par courtoisie il couvient que les amans soyent courtois et en fais et en ditz. Par prouesse il couvient que les amans s'efforcent en ce qu'ilz emprennent a faire qu'ilz n'ayent honte. Par noblesse aussi il couvient que les amans se tiennent bien nettement selon ce qu'ilz sont. Par largesse il couvient que les amans soyent larges en telle maniere que largesse leur donne renommee. Et par loyaulté il couvient que les amans soyent larges et qu'ilz ayent foy et loyauté en eulx.

L'abbesse Heloys demonstre et enseigne a son disciple que tout homme qui est ordonné et couvenable a mariage est couvenable a
145v porter les armes d'amours. Et dit que tous hommes qui / sont en
l'age de quatorze ans peulent les armes d'amours porter.

Aprés ce demonstre Heloys l'abbesse a son disciple que les sages gens aymans doyvent estre plustost receuz en la court d'amours que ceulx qu'il couvient que l'en enseigne, car chascun amant a assez a faire a garder les rigles d'amours. Mieulx vault a l'amant qu'il s'estudye a apparoir estre enseignié en l'art d'amer que il attende la doctrine

de celle qu'il ayme. Aucunesfois avient que l'amant s'esmerveille comment si grant sens peut estre en une femme que elle puisse ainsi respondre sagement aux parolles de cellui qui la requiert. L'amant demonstre par droicte raison a celle qu'il ayme que tout ce qu'il lui a dit lui tourne plus a louenge d'onneur que a blame. La doctrine d'amour demonstre que les amans si doivent entendre a acquerre la
146r grace de ce qu'ilz ayment par pur entendement / de sens et de parolles.

L'abbesse Heloys demonstre et enseigne a son disciple [que], se deux amans sont dont ly uns ait fait en son temps plusieurs biens et l'aultre nul, et soit cellui qui les biens a fait en droit eage, dit l'abbesse que celluy doit avoir plusgrant guerdon de ses biens fais que cellui qui nulz biens n'a fais. Et ce jugement est selon Dieu, car qui plus sert amour, plus digne est de la couronne que cellui qui nouvellement entre en amour. L'Art d'amour demonstre que quatre degrez sont d'amour. Le premier degré d'amour est l'entalentement d'amour de la semblance regarder de la chose qu'on ayme; le second degré est en concevant la fourme de ce qu'on ayme; le tiers degré est en l'embrasement des cuers des deux amans; le quatriesme degré
146v d'amour est en perseverance de maintenir a- / mour.[7]

Se aucun amant de bas lieu requiert noble dame ou damoyselle de noble et hault parentaige, il pourra par ces quatre degrez acquerir ce qu'il ayme. Par ceste rayson se aucun noble amant requiert amour de femme de bas lieu, il doit avoir regard que il ait temps et lieu pour acomplir ce qui affiert a amour.

L'abbesse Heloys demonstre et enseigne a son disciple que le noble amant a plusgrant grace d'amer que cellui qui est nez de bas lignage, car le noble amant se puet couvrir envers s'amye et puet faindre qu'elle lui soit ou cousine ou parente. Se la dame qui est amee est noble, elle ne se doit pas du tout arrester a la louenge de cellui qu'il ayme. Tout amant ne doit pas trop loer les fais de s'amye, les ditz, ne les parolles, car le trop parler lui peut bien nuyre. Et
147r aucune / fois advient que le trop parler tolt et oste l'embrasement des cuers des amans. L'amant dit que, qui se pourroit tenir sans trop parler, il ne souffreroit pas tant de douleur comme il seuffre par parler; mais les esperons d'amours constraignent les amans tellement qu'ilz ne se scevent contenir en l'estat d'amours sans les aguillons des parolles. Et telles choses font souvent les amans foloyer et yssir de leur voye. L'amant dit que, se la force d'amour laisse aucunefois

le cours d'aymer, la personne qui est aymee le doit souffrir, et soustenir doit le trespacement d'amour paisiblement.

La rigle d'amours demonstre que chose est apperte que amour ne
fait nulle difference entre les personnes des amans; ainçois donne a
chascune personne amant, soit noble ou non-noble, au muement
147v des drois d'amours. La rigle d'amour ne requiert four- / me ne
lignage ne beaulté, fort que la personne de l'amant a l'amye soit
couvenable a porter les armes d'armours.

L'abbesse Heloys du Paraclit demonstre et enseigne a son disciple et dit: nous veons souvent que aucunes gens qui sont ja vielz, povres, et chanuz, s'efforcent d'aymer. Et maintesfois avient que les amans ja suragez blondissent et parent leurs chiefz, en quoy jeunesse est apperceue plus du cuer que des cheveux. Nul aage ne peut tenir ne destourner le cuer du saige amant. Les bienfaiz de l'amant soustiennent tousjours son cuer en vraye amour.

Heloys l'abbesse demonstre a son disciple qu'elle ne puet par nul
certain jugement rien demonstrer a nul amant de droicte sentence
qui affiert a amant, ne elle n'a nul certain message a qui certain
148r amant puist certainement estre envoyez. Pour la- / quelle chose elle
se merveille moult comment amant terrien emprent a aymer sans
perseverer en l'acomplissement de sa voulenté. L'amant dit a l'amye:
se je me vouloye habandonner a maintenir la chevallerie d'amour,
maintes gens parleroyent chascun jour mensongeusement, pourquoy
pourroye perdre l'amour de mon amant. Et pour ce dit l'abesse
Heloys que tout amant doit acquerre le plus secretement qu'il puet
ce qu'il ayme. Et doit tout amant regarder qu'il ne gabe celle qu'il
ayme par aucunes parolles elusables, ne qu'il ne die ne face chose en
quoy elle puist avoir honte. Je diroye que les amans seroyent a
honneur s'il tenoyent ceste rigle.

L'abbesse Heloys dit et demonstre a son disciple par droicte
raison que les biens qui sont plus tost et de legiere voulenté fais sont
plus que les biens qui sont promis a venir; car tout le bien du monde
148v est de nulle valeur se il ne vient et naist / de la fontaine d'amour,
car toute naissance de bien vient de la cause d'amour. Et quant la
cause deffault, le fait va deffaillant. Nul homme ne peult faire nul
bien se l'admonnestement d'amour ne luy admonneste. Tous amans
se doivent eslargir envers ceulx qu'ilz ayment, affin qu'ilz puissent
ottroyer et accomplir l'ottroyance de leur desir. Les amans si doyvent
comme devant regarder que les personnes qu'ilz ayment soyent

vrayement confermees en bonnes meurs. Tous amans se doivent efforcer a garder tout ce que appartient a la loenge d'amour, affin qu'il donne tousjours esperance et perseverance a ce qu'ilz ayment maintenir. Lesquelles choses tous amans doivent faire a cause de pure deité.

L'abbesse Heloys demonstre a son disciple que toute largesse
doit estre donnee aux amans quant ilz sont dignes de la louenge
149r d'amour; car toute / doctrine d'amour fait les amans saiges, ja soit
ce qu'ilz soyent moult rudes a bien garder amour. Amour a telle
vertu que par la doctrine de son art elle les fait estre nouveaulx
chevalliers d'amours. Et encore demonstre l'abbesse a son disciple
que se les amans deservoyent a estre enseignez par la doctrine
d'amour, ilz acquerroyent loz et honneur; car amour a telle vertu
qu'elle donne a cellui qui est rude entendement a maintenir les
commandemens d'amour. Aucuns amans sont qui demandent comment ilz pourroyent estre saiges et introduitz a servir amour, et
comment ilz se pourroyent couvrir de la couverture d'amour. Le
sage amant dit et respont au rude qu'il ne pourroit estre bien enseignié
ne introduit en l'art d'amours se il ne tient et garde les rigles d'amours.

Amour enseigne que cil qui plus loyaulment la sert, greigneur
149v guerdon en doit avoir. Amour en- / seigne que les amans ne doivent
pas trop louer les parolles, les fais, et les contenances de celles qu'ilz
ayment, car ilz seroyent adont tenus pour flateurs, et leur nuyroyent
les biens qu'ilz feroyent ou qu'ilz auroyent fait. Aperte chose est a
amans que mieulx leur vaulsist qu'ilz se feussent detenus d'aymer
qu'ilz perdissent par leurs folz contenemens ce qu'ilz ayment.

Cy dit l'abbesse Heloys au sien disciple que, se la femme peust
ou osast acomplir sa voulenté naturelle, elle metteroit l'amour
populaire et l'amour de noblesse tout en ung poix. Mais comme la
prouesse des hommes aille devant la prouesse des femmes, femme
ne puet juger prouesse pardevant homme. Se l'amant pourpensoit
tout l'estat de son amye et dont elle est extraicte, a paine pourroit
venir a perfection d'amour. L'en doit savoir que tout amant selon
150r l'art d'amour puet congnoistre les meurs et / les prouesses de celle
qu'il ayme, de quelle noblesse, de quel art, et de quel sens elle est
aprise aux armes d'amours porter.

Chascun amant populaire, [se il] est trouvé plain de prouesse, de meurs, de grace, [et] de bonté, il doit, selon le jugement, plus estre prisié que cil qui est extrait de noblesse et riens ne vault. Noblesse

si prist premierement nom et naissance de prouesse et de l'estat du
lignage dont le premier amant vint. La naissance de la prouesse du
premier amant vint de loyaulté tout premierement, et de courtoysie,
dont tout amant noble et non-noble ont deservi d'estre receus en la
court d'amours, mais non egalement; car ja soit ce que cil du populaire
ait plus de merite en soy, il ne puet pas surmonter cellui qui est
extrait de noble lignage, car la force et aussi les richesses lui donnent
auctorité. Dont aussi l'abesse Heloys ne s'ottroyeroit pas a ce droit,
mais dit que cellui qui est noble naturellement par acroissement de
150v prouesse et de louenge, par plenté de bonnes meurs, / doit aler
devant cellui qui par richesses est noble, ja soit ce qu'il vaille mieulx.

L'abbesse Heloys dit et demonstre que tous amans doivent donner
grant esperance de vivre et de soustenir amour. Nulz amans n'ont
esperance de vivre la ou les amours leur defaillent du salut d'amours.
La rigle d'amour si dit que, quant l'amante chiet en viellesse, elle se
doubte que son aymant ne la chasse hors; pourquoy l'amante doit
respondre a son amant: vieillesse vient de nature, et n'est pas a
reprendre des fins et vrais amans, car force est, et couvient que tout
amant tourne en viellesse. Et pour ce, ja soit ce que la nature des
amans ne se puet pas tousjours tenir en ung point, on dit a ceste
cause communement: Qui bien ayme, a tart oublie.

Et encore dit l'abbesse Heloys que, quant les amans chieent en
viellesse, l'un amant dit a l'autre: J'ay moult souffert en ma jeunesse,
151r tant en souffrir, en veoir, / en desirer, en concevoir, comme en
moult de services et courtoisies; car se je les eusse a faire, je ne peusse
y fournir en ce temps. Et pour ce ces choses devant dictes considerees,
j'ay deservy a estre couronné de la couronne d'amours. Et pour ce
que je croy longuement vivre par la grace d'amour, je juge que je
suis digne de la couronne d'amour; car se je cuidasse tost mourir en
petit de temps, petit de biens pourroyent estre fais par moy.

Heloys l'abbesse demonstre et aussi enseigne a son disciple que
par droit jugement d'amours l'en doit plus loer l'amant qui plus
jecte et reçoit les javelotz d'amours sans estre occiz, ja soit ce qu'il
soit navrez et blecié, que ceulx qui riens ne sentent; car il appert que
cellui qui sert au roy du ciel dessert greigneur loyer que cellui qui
sert au roy terrien. Amours dit que cellui ou celle qui plus loyaument
151v la sert, greigneur guerdon en recevra. Et / pour ces choses devant
dictes et celles qui sont ensuivant demonstre Heloys l'abbesse a son
disciple que pour foiblesse, ne pour viellesse, ne aussi pour souffrete,

ne povreté, ne pour richesse, quoy que ce soit, amant ne doit amour laisser ne doubter.

La rigle d'amours demonstre par droite raison que sur tous les
commandemens d'amours patience est le plus fort de tous; et par
patience est amour parfaicte. La rigle d'amour nous enseigne que se
la personne qui ayme acueilt mauvais loz sans raison a celle qu'il
ayme sans deservir, il n'est greigneur douleur a souffrir. La rigle
d'amours demonstre que, tant plus que les cuers des amans sont
navrez longuement de la sayette d'amours, tant plus est l'amour de
l'amant perseverant et ferme. L'amant dit a l'amante que la playe de
la sayette d'amours est plus doulce chose a souffrir que nulle riens
qui soit. L'amant qui est de long temps navré du dart d'amours peut
152r / a paine oublier l'amour qui en son cuer est conceue. L'amant dit
que de tant comme il ne peut couvrir l'ygnorance de la personne
qu'il ayme, de tant lui croist plus douleur et paine. L'amant dit que
cellui qui ayme est en trop grant tourment quant les douleurs
d'amours il ne puet surmonter. L'amant dit que, puis que la douleur
d'amours l'a survaincu, il doit remercier amours. L'amant dit que
cellui qui ayme vrayement puet assouager par la force d'amours et
donner vie a la personne qui languist et est ja pres de mort par les
douleurs des maulz d'amours; car se l'amant s'ottroye au desirer de
l'amante, il lui donne vie et lui tolt ses douleurs, paines, et langueurs.
L'amant dit que, se l'amante lui donne remede et confort de vie, elle
le garde de la mort qui soudainement occist les amans. La rigle
d'amours demonstre que mieux vauldroit a l'amant qu'i[l] fust tantost
occiz du glaive d'amours que longuement soustenir les douleurs. La
152v rigle d'amour / fait assavoir a tous amans que trop est forte chose
a raconter les paines, douleurs, et traveilz que les cuers des amans
seuffrent. Ilz ne peuent avoir ayde de Dieu, qui demonstre que le
muet qui ne puet parler puet bien concevoir les amours, et les
demonstrer par signes.

L'abbesse Heloys demonstre et enseigne a son disciple que grant merveille est que les quatre elemens ne sont corrompus par les douleurs et par les tribulacions qu'il couvient que les cuers des amans seuffrent. La rigle d'amours demonstre que, quant l'amant est de noblesse d'amours attaint, il couvient que aucunesfois il soustiengne la forsenerie des maulx d'amours en parlant a son amye doulcement. La rigle d'amours demonstre que, quant l'amant ne se veult ottroyer a la noblesse de celle de qui il est amez, le cuer de s'amye sy ne puet

souffrir greigneur douler. La rigle d'amour demonstre que la personne qui ayme et est aymé ne doit plus demander fors que le contenement
153r d'amours lui plaise. Nul amant / si ne puet plus demander ne requerir fors tousjours garder les entalentemens de la contenance d'amours. Trestous amans doivent tousjours tendre a suivir la chevallerie d'amours, affin que par sa hardyesse il puisse deservir la couronne amoureuse.

La division de la cause d'amours ne fut pas trouvee ou temps du commencement du monde pour neant entre homme et femme, car la division requiert que tous amans maynent a fin toutes les choses qui couvenables sont aux ordres d'amours; car l'art d'amours demande a aucun amant pourquoy il est si fol que, ainçois qu'il viengne a l'acomplissement d'amours, il se rent mat et deffault.

La rigle d'amour demonstre que se la pe[r]sonne de l'amant est si nyce qu'il ne puisse pas entendre le sens des parolles de l'amante, a paine puet il avoir espoir ne confort en soustenant amours. L'amant dit a l'amante qu'il appartient au faucon et a l'austour a prendre les
153v perdriz et le fai- / sant, et non a l'escouffle, car l'oisel qui veult prendre la proye si ne doit pas voler mollement.[8] Aprés demonstre la rigle d'amours que l'amant est fol aucunesfois, quant il se prent a aymer en plus hault lieu qu'il ne doit. Et non pourtant si dit Amour: Je ne requier difference nulle ne division entre les personnes des amans, fors que elles soyent dignes et couvenables a porter mes armes. Les personnes des amans ne doivent plus requerre en la court d'amours fors que les cuers soyent onnyment navrez de la pointe du dart d'amours. Amours reçoit sans difference tous ceulx qui sont couvenables a aymer, car se les parolles estoyent vrayes que difference fust entre amans, amours ne pourroit droicturierement aler filer du fuzel d'amours.

La rigle d'amour conclud cy par sa sentence et dit que toute amour doit durer fermement entre toutes personnes sans difference. La rigle d'amours si dit et demonstre que selon [le] jugement
154r de plusieurs amans, amours doit / avoir le nom de felon juge, car qui est enlacé des maulx d'amours, il ne puet estre tenu en plus cruelle prison, selon la rigle d'amer. Car amour ne seuffre rien qui touche a vilonnye des choses qui sont couvenables a la chevallerie d'amour soustenir; et pour ce amours doit avoir le nom mieulx de doulx couraige que de felon. Amours ne reçoit en sa court nulle personne qu'il ne soit couvenable aux armes d'amours porter, s'ilz

ne sont pesees en droit poix de droicte amour, se trop fort aguillon d'amours ne les constraint. La rigle d'amour si demonstre par vive raison que, tantost comme les cuers des deux amans se accordent, maintenant est l'amour parfaicte, sans les douleurs que il couvient que les amans seuffrent.

Et encore demonstre la rigle que, ja ne sera homme si povre ne mendiant, si rude ne si nyce, ne si non-puissant, qu'i[l] ne puisse naturellement concevoir l'amour de royne ou de contesse, ja soit ce que telle amour ne se prengne pas droicturierement. Et telle amour
154v ne garde / pas la rigle d'amour, car il couvient selon la rigle que vraye amour soit conceue onnyment des deux amans.

La rigle d'amours si demonstre et enseigne [que] les amans souloyent querir plusieurs amours de plus hault ordre ou de plus bas qu'ilz n'estoyent. Et pour ceste chose aucuns amans tiennent ceste rigle d'amour, pour ce que elle ne fut pas faicte sans raison contre droit et contre nature.

L'abbesse Heloys si demonstre et enseigne a son demourant en sa discipline que par ces choses devant dictes il pert toute sa paine et si traveille en vain.[9] Tout amant doit savoir comment il doit respondre aux choses qui appartiennent a l'art d'amer. Le disciple d'amours doit louer la science de son maistre, le sens, le loz, et la prouesse, et la grant plenté de bonnes meurs; car les maistres scevent conseiller a l'art de nature, et conjoindre et amener les commandemens d'amours a droit. Nulle chose ne peut plus plaire
155r aux nobles / amantes que ce qu'elles soient arraisonnees par doulces parolles et de bons faits et de bons ditz et de bons contenemens de leurs amys.

Cy dit encore la rigle d'amours que nulle chose n'est plus griefve a nobles personnes que parolles griefves et aspres a ouyr de ceulx de son lignaige ou de sa noblesse. A ce la rigle d'amours se merveille moult que les personnes des nobles amans si se prennent a louer leur fourme et leur beaulté, ou leur prouesse ou leur lignage;[10] car tout amant est veu foloyer quant il mesmes se loue, car toute louenge vient et naist de la seulle prouesse de bonnes meurs que tous amans ont en eulx. La rigle d'amours demonstre aussi que loyaulté et prouesse prennent naissance de la racine de bonnes meurs. Et demonstre la rigle d'amours pareillement que prouesse et bonnes meurs viennent et naissent de la racine d'amours.

Heloys l'abesse demonstre et aussi enseigne a son disciple que

155v cellui qui veult avoir les guerredons de la couronne d'amours / et
estre des armes d'amours porter dignes, il couvient qu'il entre par
la porte de maulx et de douleurs. Et couvient que le cuer du vray
amant mette et jecte arriere les parolles foles du peuple mesdisant,
car le fol peuple fait ce qu'il doit, et le vray amant se doit contenir
en amour et maintenir selon sa nature. Et encore dit l'abbesse que
amours doit deffendre en toutes cours par droit tous amans en fais,
en prouesse, et en bonnes meurs.

L'abbesse demonstre et enseigne a son disciple que l'amante que
prent ne puet loyaument soutenir les estas d'amours, ne soy garder
en sa boblesse. Et en telle maniere l'estat des vrais amans est corrompu
en plusieurs lieux, et tourne a l'estat des foles amours. Tout amant
qui se vante, qui dit qu'il ait aucune chose et riens n'a, est en l'estat
de pluye ou de neige, car il n'a riens a donner dont il puisse la rigle
d'amours acomplir. Mais l'amant qui a a donner et se scet esprouver
en la grace de noblesse et de l'onneur de la court d'amours acquerre,
156r / icellui demonstre la voulenté de son cuer, et esleesse le cuer de
celle qu'il ayme. L'estat de la chevallerie de la court d'amours ne
prouffite ne ne valt a nul amant que par habondance de parolles, et
autrement il ne puet estre receu en la court d'amours par droit. Et
dit l'amant: se je suis de grant lignage, plus legierement puis estre
receu en la court d'amours, mais que soye de bonnes meurs; car de
tant comme l'amant est plus habondant en richesses et plain de
bonnes meurs, de tant doit il estre plus tost receu en la court d'amours.
Et par ceste raison monstre la rigle de droit qu'elle ne puet
certainement juger entre les estas des amans, ne contre les personnes
qui sont en amours laciees; car chascune personne des amans emporte
son faix selon ce qu'elle est. La rigle d'amours demonstre que, se
l'amant congnoist les meurs et les fais et aussi la semblance et la
contenance de celle qu'il ayme, il en est plus legier a souffrir les
douleurs du mal d'amours. La rigle demonstre que, se l'amant ayme
156v et / est plain de vertus d'amours, il ne doit pas recevoir toutes les
choses qui appartiennent a amours; car toute force d'amours vient
et naist par bonnes meurs et non par grace de lignage.

La rigle d'amours si demonstre que amant ne amante ne peuent pas bien soustenir amours que l'un ou l'autre ne soit enlacié en la mort de fine amour. Mais le chevallier est fol qui telles armes si enprent a porter, quant il ne puet souffrir les coups. Nul amant si ne puet ne doit monter sur le cheval d'amours se il n'est digne de

gouverner le cheval, car le chevallier est plain de raison naturelle et
le cheval n'a nul estat. Et telz amans sont extraitz du peuple, car ilz
ne scevent le cheval d'amours gouverner, ne la rigle d'amours garder.
Et par telz amans amours est confondue. Les coquars oultrecuidiez
et les non-francs en bonnes meurs cuident et leur semble qu'en
157r amours riens ne leur doit estre refusé. Et / dit le fol amant a l'amante
qu'elle lui ottroye toutes ses raisons estre vrayes. La rigle dit que,
se l'amante treuve son amy qu'il ne soit digne d'estre receu ou
command d'amours, et se par sa coulpe elle fait non-suffisant amy,
icelle amante et aussi sont amant peuent plainement estre gabez et
mocquez du peuple. La rigle d'amours aussi dit que, se l'amante
ottroye a l'amant ce que par fole hardyesse il demande, tout le desir
de l'amant sera acompli; c'est ce que dit la rigle d'amours. Ceste
chose ne puet pas estre mise en oubly, dit l'amante a l'amant, qui
dessus est dicte des oyseaulx de proye, de l'austour, du faucon et de
leur vol; car par leur noblesse sont leurs fais dignes d'estre loez.

L'abesse Heloys demonstre a son disciple que l'en voit aucunefois
que le faucon qui est bastard est dit faucon lasnier, et souventesfois
avient qu'il prent la perdris et le faisant pardevant le franc austour
157v ou faucon. Et ce treuve l'en par escript que ung / petit chien bien
retient ung grant senglier. Et souvent advient que le passerel enchasse
hors le mouchet, ja soit ce que le franc oysel doit avoir honte quant
la cresserelle le lieve de son lieu.[11] Doncques dit l'amant a l'amante
que par ces raisons, se il est trouvé discordable a son estat et a son
lignage en gardant les commandemens d'amours et les armes
d'amours a porter, se il est tel, il est digne de estre blasmé selon la
paresse du mol vol d'escoufle. Mais pour ce que je suis nommé estre
de la dignité du franc faucon, je ne desprise pas mon nom ne ma
nacion; car l'en ne doit pas mettre les roses ou renc des orties. Se le
besant d'or est trouvé en ung fumier, il n'est pas pour ce mestier
qu'il perde sa vertu. La lunne d'amour enlumine tousjours les cuers
des fins amans. Cellui qui bien ayme a paine vit en obscurté. Et pour
ce demonstre la rigle d'amours que nulle difference ne doit estre
158r entre les cuers des fins et vrays amans se ilz sont onnyment / navrez
des darts d'amours.

Ce nous demonstre l'abesse Heloys que la personne qui veult nouvellement entrer en la court d'amours doit entendre certainement a la chevallerie d'amours et ce qui affiert; car [selon] la rigle d'amours, amant ne amante ne doivent pas avoir regart a l'estat, aux richesses,

a la beaulté, ne aux noblesses, mais seulement a ce qui appartient a
la chevallerie de la court d'amours. L'amant et l'amante doivent
tout premierement regarder se ilz sont plains de loyaulté, de bonnes
meurs, de prouesse, et de renommee. Adoncques ces choses doivent
bien donner entendement a l'amant et a l'amante de congnoistre les
armes d'amours. Aucune fois il avient qu'amours se met en plus
hault lieu ou en plus bas que sa rigle ne requiert. Et pour ce qu'amours
si ne tient pas tousjours sa rigle, ainsi la justice d'amours
droicturierement ne doit pas estre blasmee. Il souffit tant seulement
158v a l'amante et a l'amant l'araisonnement de / belle parolle, car c'est
ce qui naturellement fait esmouvoir et sourdre l'eaue de la fontaine
d'amours. Il couvient ausi que les cuers des deux amans soyent
onnyment navrez de la sayette d'amours. Et n'est pas merveille se
la sayette navre les cuers des amans, car par la playe de la sayette les
amans deservent a avoir guerdon des paines qu'ilz seuffrent. Et se
les amans par le jugement d'amours sont trouvez contraires, ilz
doyvent estre puniz et estrangez de la court d'amours.

Adoncques si est en l'election et en la franchise de l'amant que,
quant l'amant sera aymé de l'amante, il l'aymera s'il lui plaist. Et se
l'amant ne veult aymer, il ne doit pas pourtant estre contrainte* a
aymer, selon le jugement des vrays amans; car l'amant qui ayme si
doit avoir greigneur guerredon de sa voulenté que celui qui est
contrainte* a acomplir ses amours. Et ceste rigle vient par la grace
de Nostre Seigneur Dieu le pere, qui seuffre que tous biens soyent
159r fais et tous maulx soyent laissiez / a la franchise de toutes gens, et
en donne les loyers selon ce qu'ilz ont fait de biens ou de maulx.

Toute personne qui veult aymer doit regarder moult diligemment s'elle est digne et couvenable a porter les armes d'amours. Et quant la personne est digne de porter les armes d'amours, la personne ne doit pas estre chassee de la court d'amours sans raison, s'il n'est ainsi que le cuer de l'amant ou de l'amante soit double a aymer autre decevablement. Et se l'amant ou l'amante est double en aymer, nulle raison ne les puet excuser qu'ilz n'ayent deservy a estre boutez hors de la court d'amours.

La rigle d'amours si demonstre par le jugement d'amours que a paine pourroit respondre amante ne amant aux raisons que la rigle d'amours met avant, se la grace d'amours ne lui donnoit lieu. Et

*MS: contraire

toutesfois l'amante dit selon la rigle d'amours que, se l'amant est plain de bonnes meurs et renommé de prouesse, il doit par droit estre receu en la court d'amours sans nul contredit. L'en treuve en
159v escript que / anciennement[12] l'ordre de noblesse fut trouvee ainsi comme de neant; car selon l'ordre de noblesse toute personne qui est plaine de prouesse et de bonnes meurs si doit estre reputé et tenu pour noble sans difference de son lignaige. Tout amant par droicte raison doit ensuivre selon ce qu'il est l'estat dont il est nez. Doncques tous amans ne doivent pas corrompre l'estat du lignaige dont ilz sont par mauvais vices; ainçois ilz doivent soustenir et garder l'estat et la naissance dont ilz viennent, et aussi les commandemens d'amours. Et l'estat de telz amans sera gardé aggreable et paisible entre tous amans.

L'abesse Heloys demonstre et aussi enseigne a son disciple que, ja soit ce que l'amant responde aux bonnes raisons de l'amante, toutesvoyes il se doit bien garder qu'en parlant il ne blame ou desprise
160r son lignage, sa richesse, ne sa no- / blesse, laquelle chose est forte a faire a plusieurs amans. Et pour ce que l'amante raconte ces choses dessus dictes, c'est assavoir que le faucon soit chassié de la cresserelle, toutesfois le faucon est plus digne que le vilain oysel. Mais il avient aucunes fois que le faucon lasnier par sa couardise est appellé cresserelle, car le cuer luy fault et tourne a vilonnie.[13] Et par ceste raison cy monstre l'amante a l'amant que, quant l'amant est plain de prouesse et il se met en la compaignie de ceulx qui ne sont pas de noble lignaige, il pert la grace d'amours et se met en l'estat d'amant qui est né du peuple, ja soit ce qu'il soit bien digne de la couronne d'amours. Et pour ce dit l'amante: se il n'est bien prisié et au gré du vray amant, et bien soustient amour et maintient, il n'est pas digne d'avoir la couronne d'amours.

Et pour ce que l'amante ne veult pas reprendre les moles parolles
160v de l'amant, elle demonstre par rai- / son que, se ung homme du peuple, plain de bonnes meurs, puet surmonter par sa grace l'amant qui est né de noble lieu, pourquoy ne pourra icellui du peuple, par ses* dons pris et receuz, et ses traveilz aussi souffers, estre receu en la court d'amours par le jugement de la vraye amante? Car tous amans sont nez et sont du lignaige d'Eve et d'Adam, ja soit ce que l'or et l'argent soit mieulx seant en la court d'un roy qu'en la court

*MS: ces

d'un vilain de ville champestre. L'amante preuve par vray argument d'amour que le maisgre roncin trottant porte plus souef une longue voye que l'asne qui est gras et bien amblant. Pour ce dit l'amante a l'amant qu'il se prengne garde a ceste comparoison.[14] L'amante qui bien garde et ayme l'establissement d'amours respont a son amy: ja soit ce, dit l'amante a l'amant, que ses raisons et parolles mesmement soyent souvent felles et dures, si fault que aucunement il endure pour mieulx avoir et acomplir sa voulenté. /

161r Je, Heloys, abesse du Paraclit, pour nulle riens ne me departiroye de la doctrine de mon disciple; car le vray amant dit que, ja soit ce qu'il ne reçoive nul fruit de la concepcion de s'amour, toutesfois dit l'amant que l'esperance de s'amour lui donne esperance grant temps et lieu que il espoire tousjours de venir a perseverence et acomplir la voulenté de son desir. Et souvent aussi il avient que l'esperance que l'amant a en ce que il ayme lui donne remede aucune fois par souffrance de ce qu'il requiert. Et pour ce prie je Dieu, dit l'abesse Heloys, qu'Il donne a tous vrais amans le digne loyer de leurs desertes, selon ce qu'ilz ont desservy par le droit jugement d'amours.

L'abesse Heloys enseigne et demonstre a son disciple qu'esperance doit donner hardyesse et perseverence, soustenement et confortement a tous vrays amans. Et pour ce prie Heloys que tous vrais amans puissent venir au port de salut.

161v Il / couvient, ce dit Heloys, que quant [l']amant est nez du peuple et de bas lieu, et il se veult ingerer d'aymer noble personne, qu'il ait plus de prouesse en lui que cellui qui est de noble lieu; car il couvient que tous biens et toute grace soustiennent et maintiennent l'amant du peuple, et qu'il soit subgecte a s'amye s'elle est extraicte de noble lieu.

Aprés demonstre Heloys a son disciple que, quant aucun amant de noble lieu requiert amour d'amante de plus bas lieu qu'il ne soit, il couvient selon la rigle d'amours que l'amante obeysse a son amant, selon les commandemens d'amours, et qu'elle se contiengne selon l'estat de bonnes meurs; mais ceste rigle d'amours ne tient pas par tout, car il avient aucune fois que cellui qui est extrait de bas lignage est plus plain de bonnes meurs que cil qui est extrait de noble lieu. Et en ce cas amours ne scet juger ne mettre difference entre les
162r amans, soyent du peuple / ou de noblesse. L'en ne puet trouver en ces deux cas, selon le jugement, des armes d'amours qui sont entre

homme et femme difference qui destourbe a aymer homme et femme de quelle condicion qu'ilz soyent.

La rigle d'amours demonstre et enseigne que, quant l'amant est né de bas lieu et est trouvé plain de bons fais et de bonnes meurs, le bon et noble amant s'abaisse et amenuise son loz quant il ne prent comparoison a lui, car le noble amant se doit tousjours efforcer a mieulx valoir. Se la contesse de la marche[15] ou aucune dame semblable se habandonnoit a aucun amant du peuple, tout ce ne vendroit fors d'abondance d'amour de la dame. Et tout ce monstrera l'abesse Heloys ung pou aprés, et comment amour est de telle nature et maniere qu'elle suyt tousjours le corps de sa nature. Et pour ce amour ne fait point difference, ne divise, ne ne desprise les lignaiges
162v des amans. Amour est de si franche vertu qu'elle ne de- / mande pas fors les personnes des amans, et que leurs fais, leurs ditz, et leurs contenances soyent plaines de bonnes meurs. La rigle d'amours ne requiert fors que les cuers des amans soyent droicturiers et egallement navrez des darts d'amours. Toute personne qui est amee et qui ayme se doit garder que elle soit nette, courtoise, saige, et plaine de bonnes meurs, ainçois qu'elle reprengne les estas, fais, et manieres d'autres personnes. L'en doit moult esprouver les meurs des amans, les fais, les ditz, et leurs manieres, avant qu'ilz cueillent le fruit de leurs amours; car moult de fois avient que l'amour qui est acquise par grant travail finist par achoison petite. Car aucune fois avient que entre moult d'oyseaulx aucun en est qui par sa cruaulté prent les perdriz, et celle cruaulté n'est pas selon raison ne selon nature; mais il couvient que celle cruaulté si dure jusques a ung an, et non plus ne puet durer.[16] /

163r Aprés toutes ces choses la rigle d'amours enseigne que selon l'art d'amours la noble dame se puet bien adonner a l'amour de l'amant qui est né du peuple, quant elle le treuve plain de prouesse et de bonnes meurs, sans point de difference. Et pour ce l'abesse Heloys loe et prise tous amans qui sont nez du peuple, quant ilz acquierent par vertu science et prouesse, et que par loz de bonne renommee sont enlaciez en l'amour de noblesse.

L'amante dit a son amant que icy commence son premier propoz selon l'estat d'amours; car l'amour est conjoincte entre les deux amans quant la pointe du dart les navre onnyment. Et pour ce dit l'amante a l'amant qu'elle si est appareillee a tous ses bons plaisirs, et supplie et prie que la grace de lui la vueille retenir, et que la

voulenté de Dieu si lui doint perseverence en amours, et souffrir les
douleurs, et faire chose qui soit au plaisir de son amant. Et dit
163v encore l'amante a son amant que ferme / et estable chose est que
l'esperance du travail que les amans seuffrent si ne doit pas tant
seulement estre apportee aux deux amans, ainçois doivent les deux
amans en faire partie aux nouveaulx chevalliers d'amours. Et dit
ainsi l'amante a l'amant: se la cure de mon traveil demouroit en
moy seule, je pourroye concepvoir moult de grans temptacions et
cheoir en la fin pres du peril de mort, se ainsi n'avenoit que mon
couraige fust gouverné d'esperance certaine du desir de l'amant; car
seule esperance, ja soit ce qu'elle soit couverte de decepvable couraige,
puet garder l'amante sans estre navree de l'amant.

Dit aussi l'amante a l'amant que l'ordonnement de couraige ne
reffuse donner a soy ne a aultruy service d'amours. L'en doit savoir
que aucunefois la honte que l'amante a du prendre lui tolt moult a
recevoir les dons de son amant. Aucunefois avient, dit l'amant a
l'amante, que l'amant donne a s'amye dons, non pas pour ce qu'il
164r l'ayme de cuer, / mais pour ce qu'il soit honnouré et receu pour ses
dons. Cy dit l'amante a l'amant; tu requiers que je t'ayme, non pas
pour ce que tu m'aymes, mais pour ce que tes dons et tes parolles
soyent agreables. Et par ceste raison toute vraye amante si doit fuir
tel amant. Et pour ce se tu es aourné de toutes bonnes meurs et de
toute prouesse, et dys que seulle esperance d'amour te jecte hors des
perilz de la mort, je te respons en celle maniere, que pour ce que
m'enseignes par l'art de tricherie et de decepvables parolles et par
dons descouvenables, tu requiers que je prengne et reçoive la chaleur
de luxure. Et en ce tu te demonstre[s] estre feru d'un tel baston, et
es doubles en deux choses, c'est assavoir faulce amour concevoir et
tricherie dire. Et par ce jugement, dit l'amante a son amant, la court
d'amours ne doit pas soustenir double amant, mais cellui qui est
vray en l'art d'amours, car le double amant et le decevable ne doit
164v pas par droit entrer en la salle / d'amours. Cy dit l'amante a l'amant
que quant l'amant est trouvé decevable entre les fins d'amours, il
doit estre jecté hors, car amours ne requiert que personne qui soit
couvenable a porter ses armes. Et par ceste raison dit l'amante a
l'amant: tu me admonneste[s] par dons, par parolles, et par promesses
que je m'efforce a effacer ma bonne renommee, laquelle chose me
seroit perilleuse, et me toldroit honneur. Nulle riens n'est plus
grieve que quant la noble dame oublie la grant recongnoissance de

sa noblesse et l'onneur de sa virginité par decevance de folle esperance. Et tout ce advient aux amans et aux amantes qui s'efforcent a amortir les commandemens d'amours par les folz dons qu'ilz reçoivent pour faire folie. Et telz amans ne sont pas dignes d'estre receus en la court d'amours, car entre telz amans viennent moult de perilz.

L'abbesse Heloys demonstre et enseigne a son disciple comment
165r l'amant doit / respondre a l'amante, et selon les choses proposees.
L'amant dit qu'il fait ce que amours lui admonneste, car il n'est plus
doulce chose en ce monde que vivre en bonne amour. Et dit l'amante
a l'amant: tu m'admonnestes par tes parolles que tu refuses l'amour
de moy. Je apperçoy bien pourquoy c'est. C'est pour la vile chose
qui est dicte luxure, ja soit ce que je soye renommee de prouesse.[17]
La maniere de tous amans ne puet estre contenue par les darts
d'amours en propres contenemens, c'est assavoir en ung estat et
d'une mesme voulenté, car Nature le denye. Et pour ce que Nature
le denye, nulle humaine personne ne puet estre establie en certain
estat. Nature ne clot pas les portes aux amans de certaines ordres
d'amour, se la mauvaistié des amans ne le dessert. Dit oultre l'amant
a l'amante que a tort le reprent l'amante ad ce qu'il faingne, sans
mettre au jeu de Nature, car anciennement la division d'amours fut
165v trouvee / tant seulement entre les amans qui ne sont pas dignes de
l'ordre d'amours. Et entre ceulx qui gardent la rigle de propre ordre
sont trouvez ceulx qui sont dignes d'amour et nulz autres non. Et
par ceste pourveance cy preuve l'amant que l'en treuve en la divinité
que la force de loy ne doit pas estre donnee au juste, mais a cellui
qui veult pecher. L'amant monstre a l'amante que, ja soit ce que la
division de l'ordre d'amours fust anciennement trouvee, pourtant
elle ne doit pas estre contraire aux amans qui sont dignes de la
chevallerie d'amours.

A celle fin que nulle chose vilaine ne destaingne et efface les
meurs des fins amans dit l'amant a l'amante: pour ce que je croy
certainement que esperance soit donnee a tous amans, je croy qu'elle
me doit garder de tous perilz de mort. Et monstre l'amant a l'amante
par droicte raison qu'il n'a riens proposé contre l'estat de sa glorieuse
166r grace, ne de sa loyaulté, ne pour ce / que il la vueille decevoir par
aucune faulceté, mais pour ce qu'il a declamé et si a demonstré les
concepcions d'amours, et comment il est enlacié et embrasé es
embrasemens de s'amour, et comment il avoit chier l'ottroyance de
la grace de sa glorieuse amour, et a encliné sa face aux obeyssans

d'amours. Car quant la prouesse anoblist la personne de l'amant qui est né de bas lieu, il ne s'ensuyt pas que la prouesse puist muer l'ordre de l'amant. Se l'amant est du peuple et il ayme dame noble, ja soit ce qu'il soit plain de bonnes meurs, s'il est vavasseur ou escuier, il couvient que roy ou prince lui donne celle noblesse, car autrement il ne puet estre noble appellé; car sans la grace du prince nul homme de bas lieu ne puet estre appellé noble ne recevoir la haultesse de noblesse.

Et pour ce respont l'amant a l'amante que sans raison elle prent les contenemens de son propoz a l'estat de la contesse. Et dit l'amant
166v a l'amante que l'esperance de la contesse la / deçoive, comme l'amante ne puisse par droit riens adjouster a l'estat de la contesse qui soustiengne faulceté. Dit l'amant a l'amante: tu te veulx mettre en l'ombre de celles qui portent les armes de la chevallerie d'amours, mais tu proposes moult de choses qui sont contraires a amour; car tous chevalliers amans d'amours doivent avoir soustenement en eulx, prouesse et lieu et temps, perseverent a poursuivir ce qu'ilz ont empris. Et pour ce dit l'amant a l'amante que je voy ces raisons mal ordonnees et mal baillees; je juge qu'elles ne doivent pas estre receues en la court d'amours, et juge que l'amant si peult recevoir grace de noblesse du roy ou prince quant il en est digne.

Dit l'amant a l'amante: je ne voy pas comme l'omme qui est noble ne doye porter les armes d'amours par sa noblesse; aussi puet l'omme du peuple, quant sa prouesse lui fait recevoir noblesse par la grace de ses bonnes meurs. Et par droit jugement tout homme qui
167r est couvenable a porter les / armes d'amours les puet prendre sans difference. Et par ceste raison monstre l'amant a l'amante qu'elle le reprent a tort. L'en treuve, dit l'amant, que aucunesfois es parties de France ung conte est trouvé riche de grans possessions et de grans rentes, et mal taillié de corps et mal fait de membres, et chascun l'onnoure et lui obeyst. Et est advis a tous qu'il n'ait point de prouesse, et par droit jugement les meurs de celles gens sont trouvees mauvaises, et ont fait leur nyc au coing de leur maison.[18] L'amant demonstre a s'amye que, se en Hongrie le roy est de layde fourme, les cuisses a grosses et les piez mal taillé(e)s, toute beaulté deffault en lui, mais pour ce qu'il est trouvé plain de bonnes meurs, il a deservy a porter la couronne d'amours, et court sa renommee par tout le monde.[19] Et pour ce dit l'amant a l'amante: tu ne dois pas resembler a celles qui regardent les semblances des corps; et pour ce

167v tu ne dois pas re- / garder la façon de mon corps, mais les ordon-
nemens de bonnes meurs et la renommee de ma prouesse, car de
vive nature est requis que l'en ne despise* la fourme humaine. Ne
je ne scay pas quelz biens, dit l'amant a l'amante, se glorifient. Tout
amant qui requiert amour de dame plaine de bonnes meurs acquiert
par la dame renommee de bonnes meurs.

Doncques, dit l'amante a l'amant, il couvient premierement toutes
ces choses tenir et garder a ce qu'il ait acomplissement de la chose
qu'il requiert. L'amant doit avoir regart a la droicte courtoisie de
l'amante, et comment il se pourra contenir a acquerre la grace de sa
dame. Et par ceste raison, dit l'amant a l'amante, que je te voye
introduicte en l'art d'amours, je requier ta grace et que [par] ta
doctrine me veuilles enseigner et ce qui est couvenable aux
commandemens d'amours, et tout ce qui affiert a porter les armes
168r d'amours, car / la doctrine de toy me donnera lumiere, ne ne pourray
estre aveuglez a ce que je soye desvoyé de la voye d'amours. Car
toute rigle vient et naist du ruissel de la fontaine d'amours, et tous
disciples doivent croire au conseil de leurs maistres. Et jusques cy,
dit l'amant, j'ay esté esbahy et me treuve estrangié de savoir l'art
d'amours; pourquoy l'amant requiert a l'amante qu'il soit enseigné
en l'art de sa doctrine. Et ce n'est pas merveilles, car cellui qui
requiert a avoir l'entalentement de sa pensee et qui la couvoite a
acomplir n'est pas escouté aucunesfois, ainçois est refusé de tout
quanq'il requiert.

A la quelle chose l'amant respont a l'amante et lui preuve que a
ces choses devant dictes proposees elle va contre la rigle d'amours
et contre le cours de nature; car l'amant requiert premierement
qu'il soit aymé, et l'amante lui preuve qu'il n'est pas digne de la
chevallerie d'amours. Et ceste chose monstre l'amante par droicte
168v / raison, car quant l'amant requiert a estre introduit et enseigné par
la doctrine de s'amye, il se juge qu'il n'est pas digne de porter les
armes d'amours et que la contenance de s'amour ne naist pas du
ruissel de la fontaine d'amours.

Dit l'amant a l'amante: tous amans qui ne sont pas droictement introduitz en l'art d'amours et requierent conseil, Nature leur denye; car selon le temps de l'eage dessusdit, tous amans doivent estre couvenables qui veullent prendre armes d'amours. Se les amans

*MS: despire

regardent bien et certainement les contenemens de celles qu'ilz
ayment, ilz peulent estre enseignez par la concepcion du seul regart
comme il se doivent contenir en maintenant l'estat d'amours;
autrement les amans sont tenus pour folz. Et dit l'amant a l'amante
que nulle fortresse, ne nulles armes, ne peult par droit detenir cellui
qui est digne de porter les armes d'amours. Et tous amans doyvent
169r estre plains de largesse d'amours, car / tous nobles gens amans qui
sont plains de prouesse si se doivent efforcer a acquerre ce qui est
couvenable et necessaire a amours.

L'abesse Heloys demonstre et si enseigne a son disciple que quant les amans conçoivent et voyent ce qui couvient a la largesse d'amours, ilz ne doivent pas attendre temps et lieu de faire requeste de la chose qui est acquise des parties des deux amans; car toute amour est acquise par grant tribulacion des cuers des amans, ne ne requiert pas amour que l'en lui face chascun jour requeste.

Heloys l'abbesse du Paraclit a son disciple demonstre et enseigne
que, quant les amans ne peuent avoir largesse ne habondance de
temps ne de lieu de acomplir les voulentez qui conceues sont en
leurs cuers, ilz doivent les concepvemens d'amours garder par
couraige ferme, sans entrelaissement, jusques a ce qu'ilz puissent
acomplir leurs desirs par largesse d'amour. Et doivent avoir tous
169v amans greigneur entalentement a at- / tendre la grace de la largesse
d'amour. Et pour avoir la chose qui chierement est acquise et par
grans travaulx, on a plus de merite que de celle qui est tost ottroyee;
car s'aucun voit les povres de Dieu avoir la fain et mesaise, et il les
soustient en aucune chose, il ne doit point recevoir guerredon du
seigneur pour qui il le fait. Les amans, se ilz ne peulent acomplir
leur desir, ne doivent blasmer Dieu ne ses amys et sains; ainçois
doivent prier qu'Il leur daingne donner grace que ilz puissent avenir
a ce qu'ilz requierent.* Tous amans doivent estre appareilliez a servir
toutes personnes pour l'amour de leurs amyes. Nulz amans ne
doivent mesdire a autrui, car ceulx qui sont mauldit du peuple ne
peuent estre enluminez de lumiere d'amours; car amours ne requiert
que netteté et loyaulté et honnesté, ne nulz mauvais amans ne doivent
170r recevoir prouffit de mauvaistié, ne nul villain aussi de / vilonnye.
Tous amans sont tenus a souffrir et a amender ses folies par
corrupcion de secretes parolles et de courtoysies.

*MS: ne quierent

L'abbesse Heloys demonstre et enseigne a son disciple que, quant aucuns amans ne se peuent amender de leurs folies par chastyemens, ilz ne doivent plus demourer par droit en la court d'amours; car se la court d'amours soustenoit telz amans, il sembleroit qu'elle fust consentant a les soustenir en leur folie. Tous amans qui gabent aultrui sont folz et orgueilleux et plains de mauvais vices, et doivent estre jettez hors de la court d'amours. Mais selon ce que les amans sont, ilz doivent garder nettement la rigle d'amour sans vilonnye. Tous amans se doivent garder entre les gens qu'ilz ne facent trop folz contenemens, ne trop ris, car Salomon deffent que tous saiges hommes ne nuysent de ris, car celluy qui trop rit est communement
170v tenu pour fol.[20] Et coustume si est que tous / folz amans et amantes s'entre-arresnent par mauvais contenemens et par folz ris. Car quant les amans sont trop habandonnez a ris, il semble que l'un se gabe de l'autre, et avient par ce aucunesfois que amours s'en refroide.

L'abbesse Heloys demonstre et enseigne a son disciple que a acquerre la vertu d'amour, couvient a avoir grant pourveance, et a garder droicturierement amours sans corrompance, la science des sept artz y est requise. Tous amans doivent souvent suyvre la compaignie des nobles a la court d'amours. Tous amans doivent attempreement hanter le jeu des tables, des eschetz, et des dez, et a tous les autres jeux qui ne tournent a vilonnye. Tous amans doivent recorder les fais, les meurs, et les noblesses des haulx hommes. Tous amans doivent estre couraigeux en bataille et hardys contre leurs ennemys en soustenant leurs drois. Tous amans si doivent estre /
171r sages, humbles, et moult ingenieux. Amans ne se doyvent mye enlacier en l'amour de plusieurs dames; ceulx qui sont habandonnez a aymer si doivent servir a toutes personnes, pour acquerre la grace de celles qu'ilz ayment. Amans ne doivent pas entendre trop oultre mesure a peignier leurs chiefz, ne parer leurs corps, car ainsi acquerroyent vaine gloire et laisseroyent leur deport. Les amans se doivent demonstrer sans orgueil, humbles, saiges, plaisans, et courtois. Il est adviz aucune fois a aucuns amans que ilz plaisent trop a celles qu'ilz ayment quant ilz font aucun fol fait ou dyent aucunes parolles desordonnees. Iceulx sont folz amans, et par leur nyceté sont tenus pour vilains.

Les amants qui sont saiges ne doivent pas estre jangleurs, mensongiers, ne controuveurs de nouvelles; ainçois se doivent garder qu'ilz ne parlent trop, ne que trop ilz ne se taisent. Les amans ne

doivent pas trop legerement promettre, car s'ainsi est qu'ilz
171v n'acomplissent ce qu'ilz / promettent, ilz sont tenus pour folz, et
en sont moult blasmez. Tous amans doivent recevoir a grant joye
tout ce que l'en leur donne, ja soit ce que le don soit petit, s'il[z]
ayme[nt] la personne qui le don donne, se ainsi n'est que celluy a
qui le don est offert ne croye le don estre precieux comme il soit de
nulle value. Adont cellui a qui le don est offert le peult refuser, sans
estre blasmé. Et puet dire: je tien ce don pour donné; gardez le moy
tant que je le vous demande. Laydes parolles ne doit* pas dire a celle
qui le don offre, car tous saiges amans doivent fuyr et eschever
toutes choses qui sont contraires a la court d'amours. Tous saiges
amans ne doivent gaber nul homme par fais, par parolles, ne par
faulses promesses, car toutes promesses faulses si font fol reconforter.
Tous loyaulx amans se doivent monstrer tous entiers et curiables
entre les personnes qu'il[z] veul[en]t conseiller et ayder. Nul amant
172r ne doit estre envieux des graces que / Dieu envoye a autruy.

Se [l'] amant veult estre esprouvé en la court d'amours, il doit toutes choses recevoir en son cuer, et toutes celles qui sont couvenables aux armes d'amours. Et pour ce tout amant doit rendre graces et merciz de sa doctrine a celle qui luy a apris. Mais la rigle d'amours enseigne qu'encoire ne souffist il pas a l'amant se la grace de celle qu'il ayme ne lui daigne eslargir l'entendement de l'esperance qu'il requiert, sur celle condition qu'il mettera toute cure a acomplir la doctrine qui lui est enseignee. Car l'ardeur de l'esperance que l'amant a gardera son propos pardurablement, ne ce qui est dit du trouble ordre d'amours ne puet jetter l'amant hors de son propos; car toute amour donne commencement a toute chose qui est trouvee plaine de bien, et pour ce dit l'amant que amours est racine de tous biens. Amour si doit estre par raison acquise de tous amans. /

172v L'amante respont a l'amant que tous amans doivent aprendre et scavoir, ainçois qu'ilz puissent avoir esperance de la chose qu'ilz requierent et qu'ilz la sentent prouffitable. L'amant respont a l'amante et la mercye de la grace et de la doctrine qu'elle luy a enseignee; car par raison Dieu** se humilia quant Il vout mettre en femme si grant grace de sens qu'elle puisse si sagement respondre a toutes choses que l'omme lui requiert. Et a pleu a Dieu qu'Il lui daigne octroyer plusieurs choses qu'elle propose et requiert selon

*MS: dois **MS: de soy

l'estat d'amours. Dieu lui donne voulenté de servir et acomplir son
desirer, et que elle tiengne et garde les entalentemens de sa pensee
sans deffaillir, si comme les propres meurs le requierent.

L'abesse Heloys demonstre et si enseigne a son disciple que, se
l'amant noble requiert l'amour de femme qui soit du peuple, il la
doit araisonner par telles parolles. Premierement il la doit saluer par
173r cour- / toyses parolles. Le noble amant se puet et doit seoir juxte
s'amye sans congié demander, et ceste rigle d'amours est donnee au
noble par la dignité de la noblesse. Et ja soit ce que la rigle d'amours
s'estende par droit au noble amant, dit l'abesse que ceste rigle
d'amours est donnee au noble pour la dignité de noblesse et est
generalle entre tous amans sans quelque difference; et s'estent a
condicion toute de masle et de femelle, car la grace d'humaine nature donne que le masle, de quelque condicion qu'il soit, il puet et
doit seoir juxte la femelle, selon ce qui dessus est dit, sans congié
demander.[21] Et ceste rigle tient quant il plaist a la voulenté des deux
personnes. Se les personnes des amans sont d'une semblable noblesse, il couvient aucune fois que les nobles amans requierent par
la dignité de noblesce congié de seoir juxte leur amye, car la dignité
de noblesse si le requiert. Se l'amant est de plus bas lignaige que
173v l'amante, il est en la voulenté de la grace de / l'amante a s'accorder
a asseoir son amant quant il luy plaist juxte soy.

Adoncques l'amant qui est nez du bas peuple doit arraisonner la
noble amante courtoysement, et lui doit declairer qu'il est messagier
de la chevallerie d'amours, laquelle chevallerie vous prie et requiert
que la grace de vostre doctrine le vueille enseigner et faire appertement
une doulce requeste, dont la court d'amours puist estre contente. Et
la noble amante respont ainsi a l'amant extrait du peuple et messagier
d'amours: que selon la rigle du droit d'amours elle ne puet respondre
au messaigier sans le congié du roy, comme la noble amante soit
navree du dart d'amours et l'article de la playe la touche. Et en ceste
maniere respont la noble amante au messaiger de la court d'amours,
et dit: deffendu est a tous amans que ilz ne soyent juges pour juger
en leurs propres causes. Car les choses qui retiennent les meurs de
174r la nature dont ilz naissent sont / dignes d'avoir greigneur guerdon
que les choses qui viennent de loing et dont l'en ne congnoist la
naissance. Lors la noble amante respont au messaigier de la court
d'amours que par droitte raison la couleur de la femme qui nayst
selon nature est plus digne de louenge que celle qui est fardee et

painte par art d'autrui. Et par ceste raison les parolles des gens
doivent de tant mieux valoir quant elles sont proposees que le
gergonnement de la pye.

La rigle d'amours sy demonstre au messaiger d'amours que il est
tout esbahy et esmerveillié comment l'amante respont sy sagement;
ne il ne scet se les parolles viennent de certain cuer. Et dit le messagier
a la noble amante que les raisons qu'elle met avant ne peuent pas estre
vrayement proposees par exemple du mien engin; car les choses qui
sont faictes contre nature par art d'autruy ne doivent pas par droit
174v aler devant les choses qui sont faictes selon na- / ture, car la raison
nous enseigne que nature doit aler devant l'art qui est fait d'aultrui
engin. Le messagier d'amours demonstre a l'amante que toute grace,
toute prouesse, et toute vertu vient a tous amans par force d'acquerre.
Pour ce toute personne puet acquerre amours de quelque condicion
qu'il soit, sans difference. Et l'abondance de la franchise du couraige
donne contenance d'amour a tout amant qui est digne de recevoir
amour par nature, comme a la noble amante. Doncques rent le
messager d'amour certaine response que par ce il couvient que l'amante
du peuple soit plus louee que celle du noble lieu. Le messagier dit
a sa noble amante que le faisant et la perdriz qui sont pris par le franc
oysel ou par l'austour [sont plus prisiez] que celluy qui est pris par
le huan ou par l'escouffle.[22] Ce dit le messagier d'amours que cil qui
doit recevoir doit greigneur guerdon recevoir de son creancier que
celluy qui ne rent fors ce qu'il doit. /

175r Encore demonstre le messagier par exemple certaine que le sens
et la doctrine d'un maistre doit estre plus louee que ne fait une belle
nef ou une galee bien ordonnee et bien plaisant de buches mal
ordonnees et mal taillees, que celluy qui fait et ordonne la nef de
belles buches et bien couvenables a l'(e) edyfyement de la nef ou de
la gallee. Le messager demonstre a la noble amante que la force et
le sens que vient naturellement a homme et a femme est mieulx
prisee que les choses qui viennent par le sens et par la doctrine
d'autrui. A ce enseigne le messagier d'amours que selon l'art d'amours
elle doit respondre selon la verité. Et par ceste raison l'amant respont
que l'amante du peuple va pardevant la noble quant elle l'a surmontee
par les merites de la grace d'amour. La rigle d'amour demonstre au
175v / messagier d'amours qu'il est tenu de lui enseigner la voye de la
court d'amours.

Je m'esmerveille moult, ce dit l'amante au messaiger d'amours, que toutes les raisons que tu lui enseignes si sont contre toy; car comme tu soyes trouvé plain de noblesse par la prouesse de bonnes meurs, tu estains la haultesse de noblesse par tes raisons, et fais contre toy et contre les choses aussy qui sont contenues et declairees es contenemens d'amours. Mais non! Pourtant tu te deffens par merveilleux dit d'argument. Et je m'acorde a toy, car la prouesse qui est trouvee en l'amante du peuple doit estre plus louee que celle qui est en la noble; car toute grace qui trouvee est en humble personne est digne d'avoir louenge, et doit estre plus chier tenue que celle qui vient naturellement en la personne noble. /

176r La noble amante respont ainsy au messager d'amours que grant merveille est comment grant vertu de bonnes meurs et de prouesse est trouvee en sa personne. Car il couvient que tous amans soyent jugiez droicturierement par le jugement du roy d'amours. Et par ceste raison prie l'amante que la science du messager dure tousjours sans deffault, et que telle voulenté luy mette en son cuer qu'elle puisse tousjours servir au dieu d'amours et deservir la couronne qui affiert a vray amant, et qu'elle puist avoir et acomplir ce que sa voulenté requiert.

Le messager d'amours respont a la noble amante que pas elle ne
se exaulce trop de haultesse de sa grant noblesse, quant elle s'ahert
a l'amour de l'amant du peuple; ne elle ne prent pas nom de noble
176v dame, quant elle prent amour de plus bas lieu qu'elle n'est, car / le
chevallier qui ne puet acquerir louenge en l'estat de son ordre a
paine puet acquerre loz en l'estat d'aultrui ordre. Tout amant dit
que le messagier d'amours couvient querre selon l'estat d'amours
amantes et selon leur lignaige, selon la rigle d'amours. Et ne se
doivent efforcer en autre ordre acquerre. Et se les vrays amans ne
suyvent ceste rigle, ilz doivent estre jettez hors du palais d'amours.

A ce respont la noble amante au messager d'amours que quant
l'amante du peuple est trouvee plaine de grace, de prouesse, et de
bonnes meurs, elle doit estre plus loee que l'amante qui est de noble
lieu. A ce conclut fort la rigle d'amours que quant les amours des
amans de quelque condicion qu'ilz soyent treuvent amante
couvenable, ilz se peuent par droit enlacier aussi bien en la non-
noble comme en la noble, s'elle est plaine de bonne[s] meurs, que
177r selle qui est noble et n'a que sa beaulté; et / telles amantes si doivent
estre eslevees entre les amans fins et vrays.

L'abesse Heloys demonstre a son disciple comment il doit

respondre aux argumens du messager d'amours. Ja soit ce, dit le
messagier, et afferme que l'amour de l'amante du peuple, se elle est
plaine de bonnes meurs, va devant la noble, ce dit le disciple; toutesfois
m'eslargis je, dit le disciple, et dy que l'amour de la noble doit avoir
greigneur grace que celle du peuple. Et par ceste raison demonstre
au messaiger d'amours que noble amante doit estre premierement
requise que celle du peuple; car la grace, les meurs, la prouesse, et
la noblesse vont devant les meurs de l'amante du peuple, se elle n'est
digne de trop grans merites. Et par ceste raison monstre le disciple
au messagier qu'il est contraires en toutes raisons a lui et semblable
177v a l'escrevice qui va tousjours a reculons. Tu / ottroyes, ce dit le
disciple au messagier, de nyer ce que tu affermes par la hardyesse de
ton eloquence. Mais selon droit jugement de l'umaine science, grace
sy est donnee a tout homme que il doit soustenir la science de
femme et soustenir le commencement de son malice, combien qu'il
soit saige. La rigle d'amours demonstre que, se l'amant se estudye
a rappeller sa folie, en ce* faisant il doit estre loez et estre digne
d'avoir la grace du palais d'amours. L'amant demonstre a l'amante
qu'elle ne requiert** pas l'interpretacion de ces parolles, car elle ne
les scet pas entendre; pourquoy la rigle d'amours demonstre a tous
amans qu'ilz doivent par droit entendre le jugement du roy d'amours.
Car chascun amant n'est pas digne de juger amour entre autres
amans, combien que chascun amant soit tenu a deffendre la porte
178r du palais d'amours selon sa loy- / aulté. Laquelle porte ne donne pas
entree aux amans s'ilz ne sont dignes des armes d'amours porter.

L'abbesse Heloys sy demonstre et enseigne a son disciple comment il doit respondre. Le disciple respont que, s'il ne doubtast la malice de la couleuvre, et que la femme ne le deceust, il s'estudiast voulentiers a declairer les raisons dessus dites. Mais pour ce qu'il y mettroit trop long temps, il requiert dilacion de respondre; et seroit trop grevé et pourroit par ce cheoir ou mal de la mort, se l'esperance que l'amant attendoit*** ne l'en gardoit. Le disciple dit que la dilacion de la response est amoureuse, car il couvient qu'elle viengne de la science du jugement du roy d'amours. Car en petit de temps les couraiges des amans souvent muent. Pour ce, dit le
disciple a l'amante, que se elle laisse son amant sans perfection
178v d'esperance, elle luy donne le mal / de la mort, et depuis ne luy

*MS: se **MS: requiere ***MS: attendant

puet donner medecine, ainçois puet encourir l'achoison d'homicide.

L'amante respont a l'amant que elle ne requiert ne entent faire homicide, mais raison luy demonstre que conseil requis ne doit estre denyé a celluy qui le requiert. Le messager d'amours respont au disciple de l'abbesse Heloys et lui demonstre par droit d'amours que il ne lui puet donner conseil. Et pour ce je prye Dieu qu'il puisse trouver les amours selons ce qu'il(e) requiert et avoir acomplissement de son desir.

A la quelle chose l'amant respont a l'amante: se je vouloye entendre a aymer, je deveroye requerre amant meilleur que je ne soye, car sa doctrine m'enseigneroit. A laquelle chose l'amant respont que contre amant toute amante a pure franchise d'eslire tel amant comme il luy plaist. Mais l'amant promet a l'amante que il la servira
179r toute sa vie / comme fin amant; et si se demonstrera serviable a tous pour l'amour de s'amye, car ce affiert a tous amans.

A laquelle chose l'amant respont que, se il acomplissoit ce qu'il a proposé parfaittement, il ne pourroit estre selon l'estat d'amours qu'il ne fust receu d'aucune loyalle dame pour sa loyaulté. A ce respont l'amant et prye le dieu d'amours qu'il luy donne temps et grace que a ce puisse venir. La rigle d'amours sy demonstre que, ja soit ce que tous amans ne sont pas tousjours avecques celles qu'ilz ayment, ne peuent veoir, parler, ne embracer leurs amoureuses [...][23]

L'abesse Heloys demonstre et enseigne a son disciple que, s'aucun noble amant requiert l'amour d'aucune noble dame, il la doit arraisonner par telles parolles, que puis qu'il a faicte sa requeste il doit monstrer les commencemens de son amour. Le noble amant /
179v doit ainsi parler a la noble dame: Dame, vous estes si plaine de noblesse, de franchise, et de bonnes meurs, que mon cuer est enlacié en l'amour de vous. A laquelle chose la noble amante doit respondre et dire que il dye ce qu'il luy plaira. A laquelle chose l'amant respont: ja soit ce, dit l'amant, que je presente mon corps et ma fourme au regart de vous, je ne puis pas pourtant representer mon cuer ne mon couraige a la congoissance de vostre amour. Mais l'entalentement du tresor que mon cuer desire me fait tousjours avoir regart a vostre noblesse, lequel regart me jettc hors de paine de mort et me donne confort de vie. Et ja soit ce que la largesse de dormir me deçoive aucunefois, je resve lors si doucement qu'il me semble que suys tousjours devant vostre regard. Et pour ceste vision je rens mercy a Dieu, car la vision du dormir m'oste de douleur et me donne

180r esperance de vivre en voye / de lumiere. Lesquelles choses sont
moult dignes au guerdon d'amours, car medecine donnee au mort
si ne puet donner esperance de vivre. Mais ja soit ce, dit l'amant, que
la largesse de iceste vision ne soit encore neant, j'ay esperance selon
le dieu d'amours que je recevray la deliberacion de mon desir. Dit
l'amant(e): la contenance de la franchise de la vision que le dormir
me represente ne me laissera pas longuement estre soubzmis a la
douleur de paine, ainçois croy que la grace de sa franchise me alegera
de toutes douleurs.

La noble amante sy respont selon la rigle d'amours au noble
amant, et lui monstre que la grace et la franchise d'amours l'a aprins
et introduit a respondre aux raisons dessus dictes, et recongnoist
que l'abondance de tous ses proposemens lui donnent habitacion de
repoz; car par sagesse et par concevemens de la rigle d'amours (a
180v aprins / et introduit a respondre aux raisons dessus dictes et
recongnoist que l'abondance de tous ses proposemens lui donnent
habitacion de repoz; car par sagesse et par concevement de la rigle
d'amours) le noble amant a apris tout ce a proposer. Dit la noble
amante au noble amant: il me plaist ad ce que tu m'aymes du cuer,
car tu dis et affermes [que], quant tu ne me voys de sens, tu congnois
aussy bien concepcion de m'amour comme quant tu me vois. Et
t'est advis que tu soyes present avec moy, et te prometz estre aggreable
a toutes gens pour servir pour l'amour de moy. Et par ceste cause
je suys tenue a rendre graces au dieu d'amours de la franchise de ta
noblesse.

L'abesse Heloys demonstre au sien disciple que il doit ainsi
respondre: ja soit ce que le champ qui est fait par la vertu de la pluye
181r puisse recevoir hon- / neur et vertu et aporter fruit, Nature debile
ne puet pas eschever [...][24] Mais le Dieu qui tous biens fait croistre
doit tous fruitz arouser de la pluye d'amours. Pour ce dit l'amant
a l'amante qu'elle puet bien donner a son amy arousement et
alegement de vie par les confors de vraye esperance; ja soit ce qu'elle
ne le puisse delivrer de greigneur peril que de mort, elle le puet a
toutes bonnes euvres avoyer qui l'introduisent en l'art d'amours. Et
se ainsi n'est que l'amante demonstre a l'amant sa grace, elle le met
es perilz de mort, et sy clost la porte du palais d'amours.

A laquelle chose l'amant respont: douce amye, j'ay bien entendu salutaire franchise de ta grace, et l'ayde que tu requiers de vray amant, laquelle je t'ay ja demonstre[e], c'est assavoir que tu uses

jour et nuyt de l'avision que tu as conceue; et se tu requiers greigneur
181v guerdon, tu ne le pourras impetrer a plus grant labour / que par
patience d'amour. A laquelle chose l'amant respont a l'amante: ferme
chose est et certaine que* tout mon corps si est prest a garder toute
la concepcion de mon cuer, sans requerre chose qui tourne a vilonnye;
ne ja n'avendra se Dieu plaist. Car je ne puis plus grant douleur
souffrir que je seuffre, car tous loyaulx amans qui dignes sont de
porter les armes d'amours doivent souffrir, ne ne doivent fors demander qu'ilz ayent patience de perseverer en acquerant
l'acomplissement de leur amour. Et pour ce monstre l'amant a
l'amante par ces raisons que nul vray amant ne doit estre refusé
d'entrer ou pallais de la court d'amours.

A ce respont l'amante et demande quelle chose est plus griefve
a trouver, la porte ou l'entree de la court d'amours? L'amant respont:
la plus griefve chose est a tenir continence, c'est assavoir entre les
amans qui ne sont pas trop bien introduitz en l'art d'amours, /
182r laquelle chose est trop forte a souffrir et trop griefve de departir; car
puis que le vray amant est entré en la court d'amours, il n'a pouoir
nul, car il est hors de sa franchise et couvient que la table de la court
d'amours lui administre ce que mestier lui est et chose qui soit
convenable a amant. Et telz amans ne sont pas dignes d'entrer ou
palais d'amours; et pour ce l'amant dit que la salle d'amour ne luy
fait pas convenable entree; pourquoy je te donne congié, et se tu
veulx aymer ailleurs, il te convient querre amours, car cy as tu failly.

A laquelle chose l'amante respont au congié de l'amant qu'il
n'est plus griefve chose que le departement d'amours quant l'amour
est vrayement acquise. Car la chose sy est agreable quant les amans
ne se peuent departir l'un de l'autre, car nulle rien n'est plus con-
182v venable qu'amour, car tous biens viennent et naissent / de la fontaine
d'amour. Et sans amour nulle chose n'est bien eureuse en ce monde.
Et pour ce demonstre l'amante que la salle d'amour ne doit pas estre
haigneuse aux fins amans.

A laquelle chose l'amant respont et dit que par tout la ou franchise d'amour s'estent, la vraye concepcion d'amour est acomplie. Et dit l'amant a l'amante lesquelz estatz d'amours doivent estre tenus, et lesquelx doivent estre eschevez. Dit l'amant a l'amante: se elle veult congnoistre ceste voye, elle doit souffrir paine sans fin; a

*MS: qui

laquelle chose nul ne se puet prendre, ne n'est chose plus griefve. Laquelle paine nul ne puet eschever ne souffrir sans avoir douleur, ne nul amant ne la puet raconter.

Et l'amante demande a l'amant et luy prye qu'il luy enseigne la voye de l'estat de telle paine. Lesquelx demonstremens de paine
183r font paour a tous ceulx qui les gardent, / car il couvient que tous amans soyent navrez du dard d'amours. L'amant sy respont que les dartz qui sont premierement veu(e)s sont plus legierement eschevez que ceulx qui sont reposez ou sentier d'amours. Et dit l'amant que les darts ne blescent pas, ceulx qui sont veuz, comme ceulx qui ne sont pas veuz. Et dit l'amant a l'amante que s'il luy plaist savoir les paines d'amours, il lui couvient ainçois qu'elle ait soulas de ce qu'elle desire, car le pallais d'amours est assis ou milieu d'amours. Et couvient que par paine tous amans y entrent. Et ou pallais d'amours a quatre parties gracieuses, et en chascune partie a quatre portes assises. En chascune partie du palais d'amours sont dames et chevalliers, qui ont acquises les armes par la dignité de souffrir. La premiere porte du pallais tourne vers orient et est tousjours ouverte a la royne d'a-
183v / mours. Le regart des portes attrayent tousjours les bons chevalliers d'amours par leur delectableté. Deux des portes sont ordonnees a l'entree de l'ordre des dames. Ausquelles choses l'amant demande quelle porte est celle qui est tousjours ouverte et est tousjours assise en la charniere des gens? C'est la porte du palays d'amours, que toute personne amant requiert entrer qui est digne des armes d'amours porter.[25]

L'abesse Heloys demonstre au sien disciple que une dame estoit de trop noble semblance et de tresgrant noblesse nee, et chevauchoit ung bien maigre cheval, clochant de quatre piez. Lors elle appella ung messager par son droit nom et lui prya qu'il venist a elle, et il y vint. Sy tost comme il vint a elle, il descendy et la salua, et lui offry son cheval, qui estoit plus beau que le sien. Mais la dame ne le voult
184r prendre. Adont / se print la dame a araisonner le messagier par teles parolles: Messagier, tu qui serches* ton seigneur; il n'est pas cy, tu es ja trop eslongié de lui. Adont prya le messager la dame que par amour et par sa grace elle luy daignast demonstrer la voye par laquelle il puisse trouver son seigneur. Auquel la dame respondy qu'elle ne lui pouoit enseigner. Aprés dit le messager: Dame, enseignez moy

*MS: sers

quelle compaignie de chevalliers est ce que je regarde; et par quelle raison, dit le messager, portez vous sy letz paremens, comme vous soyez de belle fourme? Auquel la dame respondy: Messager, je te diray: les appareillemens signifient batailles de chevalliers de mort.*

Quant le messager ouÿ ce il conceut courroux en son cuer et lui
en palist la face. Adont se departy le messaiger de la dame et de l'ost
184v qu'il avoit veu. Et ne / veult la dame donner nul confort au messager.
Adont lui prya le messager courtoysement que s'il luy plaisoit, elle
le pouoit garder de mort. Et la dame eut lors pitié de lui et lui dit
qu'il demourast avec elle et il seroit hors de peril. Le messager a la
requeste de la dame demoura; et elle lui demonstra les enseignemens
des choses qu'il avoit veues. Messager, dit la dame, les chevalliers
que tu as veus conduysent le dieu d'amours estre droit en son verger. Ne ne puet le dieu d'amours estre veus que ung jour de la
sepmaine; et ce dieu sy donne a chascun amant guerdon selon ce
qu'il a desservy. Toutes dames qui sont aornees et plaines de bonnes
meurs sy ont leur mancion ou vergier d'amours en delectableté,
selon les paines que elles ont souffertes a maintenir amours.
Chevalliers d'amours gouvernent le pallais et servent le dieu
185r d'amours, chascun selon son / ordre. Ces autres dames que tu voys,
ce sont celles qui ont esté corrompues en maintenir amours par les
dons des faulx amans et de folz requerans. Et pour ce seuffrent elles
les tourmens dehors le vergier d'amours, car la porte du verger
d'amours n'est ouverte a nul fol amant. Celle autre compaignie de
dames que tu voys la dehors le verger sont dames qui ont esté sy
viles et si desnuees de tous biens que oncques ne virent les portes du
pallais d'amours ouvertes. Tous amans qui deservent la gloire du
dieu d'amours regnent en gloire et en delectableté ou verger.

Le messagier mercya la dame de ce qu'elle lui a monstré
l'ordonnance du verger d'amours; et prye a la dame qu'elle luy
donne congié d'aller querre son seigneur, et promet au dieu d'amours
qu'il racontera a tous amans l'ordonnance du vergier. A ce respont
185v la dame au / messagier qu'elle ne lui peult donner congié sans le
commandement du dieu d'amours, et qu'il ait souffert grans paines
et grans travaulx; et qui icelles souffrera, il acquerra les graces de la
chevallerie d'amours.

Endementiers que la dame et le chevallier messager parloyent

*MS: damours

ensemble, ilz entrerent en trop beau lieu environné de bois, de prez, de vignes, et de rivieres, et de toute delectableté qui affiert a cuer d'amant. N'oncques homme mortel n'avoit veu plus beau lieu. En ce lieu estoyent toutes manieres d'arbres, et portoyent fleur et fruit. En cellui lieu croissoit mierre moult souef, qui donnoit grant oudeur et umbre aux chevalliers et aux dames d'amours. En celluy verger naissoit une fontaine, qui estoit de telle doulceur et de telle bonté que elle assouagoit tous malades et donnoit appetit a tous descou-
186r / ragés. Juxte icelle fontaine seoyent le roy et la royne d'amours en
ung trosne aorné d'or et d'argent et de pierres precieuses. Et chascun d'eulx avoit une couronne d'or resplendissant, et estoyent vestus de nobles paremens, et tenoyent chascun en sa main une verge doree. Nulz homs n'osoit asseoir pres d'eulx. D'encoste le roy et la royne avoit une voye qui menoit tous amans en delectableté, ne ne sentoyent nulle douleur.

Quant la dame qui le maisgre cheval chevaulchoit et le messager vindrent a la porte du verger d'amours, le portier vint et les mist ens et leur monstra la voye de la fontaine du verger. Et virent le roy qui tenoit une harpe de cristal en sa main. Et virent grans compaignies de chevalliers et de dames entour le roy. Et chascun estoit bien appareillié noblement selon son ordre. Chascun chevallier eslisoit
186v siege tel comme il le vouloit. Ha! dit dont la dame, cy / a grant
gloire et grant grace que telle gent ont desservye. Ne nulle langue ne pourroit raconter la noblesse du verger. Pardevant la chevallerie d'amours jongleurs y jouoyent de toutes manieres d'instrumens; et y estoyent damoyseaulx et damoyselles prestz de tout service faire, appareillez chascun selon son estat.

Tant alerent ensemble la dame et le chevallier qu'ilz desendirent delez la fontaine d'amours; laquelle fontaine ilz ne peurent passer. Adont s'arresterent et lacherent leurs frainz et s'assirent juxte ung bel arbre. Adont virent la dame et le chevallier tourmens de diverses manieres. Et griefve chose seroit de raconter toutes les paines qu'ilz souffroyent; desquelles* paines acqueroyent soulas par pascience de les souffrir. Aprés ceste compaignie d'amans ilz virent de rechief
187r une compaignie qui ne souffroyent pas douleur, ainçois / estoyent
en joye et en soulas. Adoncques monterent la dame et le chevallier et vindrent a la porte du verger d'amours et ne peurent passer.

*MS: lesquelles

Aprés ilz virent une compaignie de dames en siege, dont chascune avoit ung faissel d'espines sur quoy elle seoit, pour souffrir plus grant paine, car les pointes des espines les tourmentoyent.

Quant le chevalier eut veu toutes ces choses, il demanda congié, et la dame qui le maisgre cheval chevauchoit lui respondy qu'elle n'avoit pouoir de lui donner congié. Mais je te loe, dit la dame, que tu laisses cy ton cheval et te haste[s] a querre la voye du verger d'amours, par laquelle voye le roy d'amours y entra, et luy requiers congié comme a ton seigneur de t'en aler. Et sy te loe que tu mettes paine a acomplir ce qu'il te commandera. Et sy te prie et requier que vers lui tu pries pour l'amour de moy. Adont dit le messager au roy
187v d'amours que il le / regracioit et mercyoit de ce qu'il avoit veue la haultesse et la noblesse du vergier d'amours. Et dit en la fin le messager qu'il estoit prest a servir au roy et a la royne et a amours tant comme il vivra.[26] Adont prist congié et yssy du vergier et revint a son maistre.

Cy finent les epistres de l'abesse Heloys du Paraclit, laquelle abaye maistre Pierre Abaielart fonda ainçois qu'il mourust. Et ensuyvent les demandes en amours.

188r

LES DEMANDES D'AMOUR

1. Du chastel d'amours il convient
Que me nommez le fondement.
Loyaument aymer

2. Aprés nommez le maistre mur,
Qui plus le fait fort et sceür?
Bien celer

188v
3. Dittes moy qui sont les carneaulx,
Les sayettes et les carreaulx?
Regarder et attrempance

4. Je vous demande quelle est la clef
Qui le chastel peut deffermer?
Prier sagement

5. Nommez la sale et le manoir
Ou l'en puet premier joye avoir.
En bel acueil

6. Quelle est la chambre ou sont ly lit,
Ou l'amant prent son premier lit?[27]
Jouyr oultreement

7. Aprés les gardes me nommez
Par qui le chastel est gardez.
Vivre lyement, vestir gentement

8. Qui fait aux fins amans jouyr
De ce dont ilz ont grant desir?
Bien parler

9. Qui fait amours long temps durer,
Et enforcer et embraser?
Courtoysie

10. Dont puet greigneur prouffit venir
189r En fines amours maintenir?
En bien celer

11. Qu'est en amours grant courtoisie
Mains prouffitable et plus prisie?
Ung doulx baisier

12. Quelle est la moindre chose qu'amours face,
Qui plus conforte et fort solace?
Un doulx regard

13. Qu'est en amours grant courtoysie
Que nul ne la reçoit qui rie?
Bel escondit

14. Par quel savoir, ne par quel chose
Du cuer ou de la bouche close,
Puet myeulx saige dame esprouver
Celuy qui la prie d'aymer?
Par dangier

15. Qu'est en amours mere et nourrice,
Tant plus est noble, tant plus est nyce?
Esperance

16. Amye, amant, qui aymer vault,[28]
Quel chose est ce que myeulx lui vault,
Et au plus grant besoing lui fault?
189v Bien parler

17. Dy moy d'amours le dart vilain,
Tant plus me fiert, et je plus l'aym,
Tant plus me fiert vilainement,
Je plus l'endure legierement.
Faulx semblant[29]

18. Quelle est l'enseigne par* dehors,
Qui plus monstre l'amour des cors,
Et est l'enseigne si apperte,
Qu'elle ne puet estre couverte?
Muer couleur

*MS: plus

1. Beau Sire, je vous demande lequel vous aymeriez le myeulx, ou a jouyr sans desirer, ou a desirer sans jouyr?

Dame, j'auroye plus chier a desirer sans jouyr.

Sire, pour quoy?

Pour ce, dame, que celluy qui jouyst sans desirer et sans sentir
190r aucune / paine si ne scet quelle* est parfaicte amour, ne sy ne scet
dicerner le bien du mal; ne il ne sent mye le grant honneur qui descent de loyal desir ne d'espoir d'avoir mercy; car le noble don d'amours est engendré par desirer, attempré et arrousé de plaisance.

2. Beau Sire, je vous demande lequel a il plus, ou de vous en amours, ou d'amours en vous?

Dame, il y a plus d'amours en moy; car la vertu d'amours est si grant et si puissant que la noblesse d'amours est parfaictement en tout cuer loyaument desirant. Et de ce me doivent croire tous loyaulx amans, car ainsi est.

3. Beau Sire, je vous demande du quel loyal amant treuve plus en amours, ou du bien, ou du mal?

Dame, plus de bien; car nul ne nulle ne puet en amours tant d'ennuys endurer que ung tout seul bien n'estaingne tout. Et quant l'amant a eur et grace d'attaindre le mercy de sa dame et recevoir
190v nom / d'amy, lors sont tous ses ennuys et maulx convertiz et tournez
en parfaicte joye. Et croyez qu'en vraye amour n'a nul amer, ne oncques loyal amy mal ne senty pour loyaument aymer.

4. Beau Sire, je vous demande se joye croist plus en cuer de fin amant par vray espoir que par vray desir?

Dame, espoir est le plus grant bien d'amour aprés mercy; car loyal desir et doulx penser naissent d'espoir, et par vray espoir et par vertu de gracieux souvenir vraye amour est engendree.

5. Beau Sire, s'il est ung homme que deux femmes pryent d'aymer, et longtemps leur a donné a entendre qu'il les ayme et a aymees, et est ainsi que l'une l'ayme en bonne maniere, et moult vouldroit son honneur et son prouffit et aussy, si comme elle dit, l'avancement de luy, et aprés (ce) l'ottroy fait par semblant ou par fait il ne treuve
191r en elle / nulle certaineté en maniere que le fait s'acorde a la parolle,
ainçoys y treuve tout le contraire; et l'autre escondit tousjours son

*MS: qui

amour, mais en escondissant ung doulx regard, nourry de leesse et enluminé d'un gracieux riz floury de doulceur, descent de ses yeux amoureux, qui par advis luy donne esperance de venir a s'amour et tousjours, combien qu'elle l'escondisse par doulx semblant et amyable, en laquelle se doit il plus fyer, et laquelle cuidez vous qui myeulx l'aymast?

Dame, il doit avoir plus grande affection en celle qui en escondissant le regarde de ses beaux yeux amoureusement, car le regard naist du cuer par fine amour. Et doit esperer l'amant que celle qui l'escondit sy le fait pour son honneur garder. Et celle qui luy ottroye s'amour et puis y treuve le contraire du fait, celluy ottroy ne naist mye de bon fait du cuer, sy comme il appert par parolles subtiles et couvertes. /

191v 6. Beau Sire, je vous demande lequel vous aymeriez mieulx, ou a oyr dire moult de biens de vostre amye et vous y trouvissiez mal, ou que vous en ouyssiez dire mal et vous y trouvissiez du bien?

Dame, j'auroye plus chier que je en ouysse bien dire et que je y trouvasse mal, pour ce que avancié je ne puis estre ou son bon los est amendry. Et pour chose que je sente en la servant je n'en perdray ja l'espoir que j'ay d'avoir l'amour d'elle.

7. Beau Sire, s'il estoit ainsy que vostre amy[e] vous eust ottroyé dix baisiers, et jamais plus rien eussiez d'elle, je vous demande se vous les prendriez tantost, ou se vous attendriez longuement?

Dame, je ne les prendroye mye tantost, ainçois m'en devroit tousjours ung ou deux, pour ce que l'en ne doit mye despendre tout le bien que l'en a a ung coup; et se j'avoye prins tous les dix baisiers
192r qu'elle m'avoit donné pour le gré / d'amours d'elle, je seroye hors bouté, ne jamais vers elle n'oseroye retourner.

8. Beau Sire, se vous estiez en ung lieu secret avecques vostre amye, lequel auriez vous plus chier, ou que vous alissiez vers elle et la baisissiez par une foys de son gré sans plus, ou qu'elle venist vers vous ses bras tendus pour vous acoller et baisier, mais ainçoys qu'elle y peust estre venue, pour aucun qui feust survenant luy* couvenist retourner?

Dame, j'auroye plus chier qu'elle venist a moy les bras tendus,

*MS: la

pour ce que cent fois plus me devroit plaire ce que seroit de sa propre voulenté que quanque je pourroye faire; car nul ne puet sy bien joye faire sentir comme celle dont l'en desire a jouyr.

9. Beau Sire, il est ainsy qu'il sont deux qui ayment deux dames, dont l'un parle toutes les fois qu'il veult a celle qu'il ayme, mais elle
192v luy dist / tousjours qu'elle ne l'ayme point et que ja ne l'aymera, et l'autre ne puet parler a celle qu'il ayme, ains est enfermee en une tour, mais une fois a la XVe ou le moys la puet veoir par une fenestre et la saluer tant seulement, et bien est certain qu'elle l'ayme tant que femme puet aymer homme; je vous demande lequel doit estre plus conforté d'amours, et qui plus se doit en esjouyr?

Dame, celluy qui ne puet parler a sa dame, pour ce qu'il a en ce tout ce qu'il puet demander en amours: c'est mercy, lequel il a quant il est amé d'elle. Et celluy qui parle a s'amye sans nul confort trouver frit et art du feu amoureux, lequel il esprent et si le alume tout par l'approucher. Si lui vaulsist myeulx qu'il s'en tirast arriere, car certain est qu'il pert sa paine.

10. Beau Sire, il sont deux seurs, tou[te]s d'une beaulté et d'un
193r sens. Vous en aymez l'une tant comme homme si / puet aymer femme, et elle ne vous ayme point; et l'autre vous ayme, et vous ne l'aymez point. Et l'une scet la voulenté de l'autre, et vous mesmes savez leurs voulentez. Si advient qu'elles sont en une eaue avecques vous, et couvient que vous en noyez l'une; je vous demande laquelle vous noyeriez?[30]

Dame, celle qui m'aymera et que je n'aymeray point, pour ce que je ne seroye mye loyal amy, et pou se pourroit on fyer en moy, se je noyoye celle que je aymeroye tant. Ce ne me pourroit avenir, car trop je seroye mauvais; et j'auroye espoir que pour luy faire loyaulté que elle verroit en moy, que pitié arrouseroit son franc cuer de plaisance, si que mercy y nourriroit par la vertu de loyale amour, dont si tresparfaicte honneur descend.

11. Beau Sire, je vous demande lequel vous aymeriez myeulx, ou que vostre amye mourust, ou qu'elle se mariast a aultruy?

193v Dame, j'aymeroye mieulx qu'elle se ma- / riast, pour ce que je la pourroye aucune foys veoir; et combien qu'elle fust maryee, sy ne la lairroye pourtant a aymer de vraye amour, ne ja n'en perdroye le myen espoir.

12. Beau Sire, je vous demande, se vous aviez ung loyal compaignon qui bien vous aymast, et vous aussy luy, lequel auriez vous plus chier, ou qu'il preist vostre amye a femme, ou que vous prenissiez la sienne?

Dame, j'auroye plus chier que je prenisse la sienne, pour ce que combien que je eusse son amye espousee, je ne laisseroye ja a aymer la myenne. Ainsy je l'aymeroye en jouyssant de la sienne, et sy auroye espoir de avenir a l'amour de la myenne. Et ainsy pourroye je jouyr des deux.

13. Beau Sire, je vous demande quelle* est la courtoysie qui
194r puet estre en amour sans penser, sans espoir, sans / jouyr, sans [desir]?[31]

Dame, c'est que l'en fust amez et que l'en ne le sceust mye.

14. Beau Sire, je vous demande laquelle amour vault myeulx, ou celle qui** de long temps est desiree, ou celle qui de legier est ottroyee?

Dame, celle qui desiree est longuement, pour ce que comme plus est la chose desiree et myeulx plaist, et plus y treuve on d'amour et de joye quant on l'a. Et lors multiplie celle amour en tous parfais biens.

15. Beau Sire, je vous demande laquelle amour est plus sceüre et durant plus, ou celle qui est legierement donnee, ou celle qui est long temps desiree?

Dame, celle qui est longuement desiree, pour ce que comme l'en a plus desiree l'amour, de tant mieulx la garde l'en quant on l'a.

16. Beau Sire, je vous demande, ou il a plus grant sens a garder
194v amour / et mercy quant l'en l'a acquiz, ou a amour acquerre et mercy?

Dame, il y a plus grant science a garder sy parfaitte honneur, qui la puet avoir.

17. Beau Sire, je vous demande quelles sont les trois choses par quoy l'en garde myeulx amour et mercy?

Dame, sens, loyaulté, et celer, car par sens est amour concquise, et maintenue par loyaulté, [et] couverte et gardee des mesdisans par bien celer.

*MS: qui **MS que

18. Beau Sire, je vous demande quelles sont les deux choses qui plus fort confortent loyal amy en aymant?

Dame, espoir et souvenir, car bon espoir de venir a son desir luy
arrouse son cuer et le syen desir par plaisance, et souvenir lui envoye
doulx espoir et le fait penser a parfais biens qui naissent a servir
amour. Et en pensant luy est advis qu'il voit le gent corps de s'amye
195r par la vertu de savourer espoir de mercy. Ainsy il est / conforté et
nourry en joye.

19. Beau Sire, je vous demande lesquelles deux choses font plus de mal en aymant a loyal amy?

Dame, desir et paour, car desir luy court si appertement sus qu'il ne puet nuyt ne jour durer, et paour sy ne lui laisse descouvrir ne dire son estat a sa dame pour doubte des envieux et des mesdisans, et pour la cremeur d'estre esconditz ou de mesparler.

20. Beau Si[r]e, je vous demande se le loyal amant doit laisser l'aymer pour mesdisans ne pour escondit?

Dame, nennil, ains doit souffrir et attendre sagement, et tousjours pryer et demander mercy et grace de sa dame. Et doit mettre toute son attente a faire tant qu'il puist en aucune maniere plaire a sa dame et amye.

21. Beau Sire, il est vray que amours a grant puissance sur tous
195v bons et loyaulx cuers, et aussy sur tous autres, / et puet tous durs
et faulx cuers ravoyer et faire amans. Or vous demande je pourquoy
elle ne fait les mesdisans aymer, sy que on n'eust point d'envye sur
les amans?

Dame, pour ce que amours ne doit avoir cure que ja mauvais ayent le nom d'amy, ne qu'ilz jouysse[nt] de ses* grans biens; car se estoit ainsy que amours donnast a tous puissance d'aymer onnyment, nul ne congnoistroit les doulceurs ne son bon temps, car nul ne scet que biens sont qui oncques mal ne senty.

22. Beau Sire, je vous demande s'il est bon que mesdisans soyent en amour, et s'ilz font nul prouffit aux amans?[32]

Dame, oyl, car les vrais amans sy en deviennent plus saiges et mieulx avisez, plus souffrans et myeulx attrempez. Et s'il avient que

*MS: ces

ilz leur facent mercy et le noble don d'amy, tant y treuvent ilz et
196r ont plus de / doulceur, quant ilz ont grace de l'avoir.

23. Beau Sire, je vous demande lequel amant vault myeulx a aymer, ou le hastyf et hardy, ou le souffrant couart et doubteux, pour ce que hastive voulenté ne hardement n'ont mestier en amours?

Dame, le souffrant couart vault myeulx, car attrempee voulenté, couardise, et crainte y affierent pour garder l'onneur et la paix de sa dame; car loyal amy se doit tousjours doubter des mesdisans et de mesparler, especiallement de faire ou de dire chose dont l'onneur de sa dame soit ou puist estre amendrie.

24. Beau Sire, s'il estoit ainsi que ung homme aymast vostre amye, je vous demande lequel vous aymeriez myeulx, ou que vous l'encontrissiez a l'entree et il en ven(s)ist et vous y entrissiez, ou qu'il y entrast et vous y yssissiez?

196v Dame, j'auroye plus chier qu'il en yssist et je / y entrasse, car je ne pourroye estre joyeux ne a[voir] la paix de mon cuer, s'il estoit demouré avec ma dame, et je le sceusse. Et se je y estoye demouré et il s'en fust alé, j'auroye espoir de tout deffaire ce qu'il auroit fait et dit par couvertes et soubtiles parolles.

25. Beau Sire, ilz sont deux amans; l'un est en son venir et commence a aymer, et l'autre jouyst de l'amour de sa dame. Je vous demande lequel vit plus liez et joyeux, et plus amoureusement?

Dame, cellui qui nouvellement commence; car arbre qui est vert et floury est en sa plus grant beaulté, et sy tost que le fruit est vieux et cueilly, son meilleur temps est passé, et a perdue toute sa verdure. Aussi cellui qui jouyst de ses amours a perdu le deduit, le glay, et la doulceur d'espoir et de souvenir, et la doulceur aussi de penser aux parfais biens qui naissent de servir amours en esperant le gracieux
197r ottroy de mercy qui le tient gay, chantant, / et reveleux.

26. Beau Sire, je vous demande se vous estes plus conforté et enflambé de l'amour de vostre dame en la regardant que en pensant a elle?

Dame, nennil, car aussy tost comme je la voy, je suys sy trespensyf et transy en son amour que j'en deviens comme muet et esbahy. Et quant je suys bien ententif a parfaictement penser a elle, il m'est advis en pensant que je voy devant moy son gracieux corps, sy que le doulx penser d'elle est tout mon deduyt et mon confort.

27. Beau Sire, je vous demande lequel est le greigneur bien d'amours?

Dame, doulx mercy, floury de joye, paré de grace, enluminé de plaisance, et gouverné d'onneur.

28. Beau Sire, je vous demande comment est il, quant amant a mercy de sa dame, s'il puet autre chose demander a amours?

197v Dame, oil: sens et vou- / lenté de savoir garder et maintenir si parfaitte honneur et le grant bien qu'amours luy a donné pour le servir soingneusement.

29. Beau Sire, je vous demande quelle chose est mercy?

Dame, mercy est amour ottroyee, et de mercy naist le tresnoble don d'amours floury de parfite joye.

30. Beau Sire, je vous demande qu'est amours?

Dame, c'est une vertu invisible, dont la substance et les euvres monstrent la voulenté et maniere d'aymer. Et commence amour par regard.

31. Beau Sire, je vous demande qu'est meilleur en amours, ou sens ou celer?

Dame, sens, car loyaulté et celer sy naist de sens, ne nul ne puet savoir le celer se n'est par la vertu de sens, lequel gouverne amours.

32. Beau Si[r]e, je vous demande lequel vault mieulx en amours, ou sens ou loyaulté?

Dame, sens, car loyaulté vient de foy, qui est le chief de tou- /
198r tes vertus. Et de loyaulté naist sens, et par sens est engendree voulenté, qui a pouoir de faire gouverner amours par loyaulté.

33. Beau Sire, je vous demande se beaulté est la vertu par quoy l'en ayme plus tost?

Dame, oyl, communement pour les delitz naturelz que les cuers desirent, mais les saiges ayment ainçois pour sens que pour beaulté.

34. Beau Sire, je vous demande se hommes ayment plus pour sens que pour beaulté?

Dame, beaulté est la mendre des vertus. Neantmoins c'est la plus desiree, tellement que par beaulté plusieurs sont espris d'aymer; mais les saiges qui tendent a honneur ayment ainçois par sens que par beaulté.

35. Beau Sire, je vous demande se femme se doit plus esjouyr pour beaulté que pour sens?

198v Dame, elle se doit plus esjouyr pour sens que pour / beaulté; et si est il moult de femmes qui plus chier auroyent a estre belles que saiges.

36. Beau Sire, je vous demande s'amours commencee par beaulté dure plus que celle qui est commencee par sens?

Dame, celle qui est commencee par sens est plus durante, car sens dure plus que beaulté.

37. Beau Sire, je vous demande lequel auriez vous plus chier, que vostre amye fust belle et pou savante, ou qu'elle fust saige et pou belle?

Dame, sage et pou belle. Non pourtant sy me plairoit elle plus belle que laide, mais pou vault beauté s'elle n'est paree de sens.

38. Beau Sire, je vous demande quantes manieres de desirs a il en amours?

Dame, quatre desirs naissent* de sa vertu.

Quelz sont ilz?

Dame, le premier est que l'en ayme pour honneur et pour mieulx
199r valoir, le second est pour avoir s'amye a femme, le tiers / pour aucun avantage, et le quart faire sa voulenté de s'amye.

39. Beau Sire, je vous demande lequel de ces quatre desirs vault le myeulx?

Dame, le premier, pour honneur et pour myeulx valoir, car toutes gens de quelque estat qu'ilx soyent, peuent myeulx aymer de ce desir sans pechié et sans amenrir leur honneur ne leur estat.

40. Beau Sire, je vous demande pourquoy amour est ou fut establie?

Dame, pour multipliance de joye et du monde, pour doctrine, et pour apprendre a venir a grant honneur ceulx et celles qui ayment de fines et vrayes amours, et pour accroissance de tous biens et de parfaitte joye, nourrie en soulas et en deduyt, dont il ne seroit point se amours ne fust; donc d'elle naissent ces vertus.

*MS naissans

41. Beau Sire, je vous demande se en amours a point de fin?
199v Dame, nennyl, car vraye amour ne puet ne / [ne] doit finer, et tousjours fut et est et sera pardurablement.

42. Beau Sire, je vous demande, s'il estoit ainsy qu'amours peust ne deust finer, que devendroit elle?

Dame, elle iroit a Dieu, dont elle vint; car pour vray a droit juger je dy qu'amours est Dieu, et est et fu et sera le plus loyal Amant qui oncques fust, ne qui jamais soit, car Il mourust par amours. Et pour ce le doivent tous et toutes amer, honnourer, et servir.

43. Beau Sire, je vous demande laquelle amour est la plus asseüree, ou celle de regart sans dire, ou celle qui est ditte de bouche et descouverte?

Dame, celle qui est ditte de bouche.

44. Beau Sire, je vous demande et pry par la force du jeu que vous me dittes verité, dont vient amoureux regart?

Dame, il naist de cuer.

200r Et, Beau Sire, puis que amoureux regart / vient du cuer, je vous prye que vous me dittes cause pourquoy l'amour qui commence par regart n'est aussy sceüre comme celle qui commencee est par la bouche?

Dame, pour ce que l'en se doit tousjours doubter de la personne qui est acoustumé d'amoureusement regarder.

45. Beau Sire, je vous demande, se ung homme appercevoit que la femme qu'il ayme soit coustumiere de faire amoureux regars, et il ait espoir qu'elle ait bonne voulenté vers luy, se fy[e]ra il en son regart tant qu'il luy doye descouvrir sa voulenté toute?

Dame, ouyl, s'il la voit tousjours perseverer ainsi (perseverent) en son regart, car amoureux regars et continuelz tousjours viennent d'amoureuse voulenté.

46. Beau Sire, je vous demande, quant l'amant sent la voulenté et la valeur de son amye, pourquoy est il donques jaloux?

200v Dame, pour ce qu'il se doubte / que aucun ne face ou dye chose par quoy il puist ou doye estre eslongné de son amye, et qu'elle ne soit esprise d'autre amour en aucune maniere aultre que luy; car femme de sa nature oit legierement ce qui tourne a la louenge d'elle, si que par aucuns flateurs est aucunesfoys l'amy eslongné de s'amye, et souvent il advient ainsy.

47. Beau Sire, je vous demande dont jalousie vient en amours?
Dame, de trop asprement aymer, et de souspeçon. Et aucuns ont dit et dyent qu'elle vient de sottye, mais je ne m'y puis ne ne m'y vueil accorder. Neantmoins ce n'est mye sens.

48. Beau Sire, je vous demande, se ung amy doit estre jaloux de son amye, ne l'amye de son amy?
Dame, nennil, fors pou ou neant, mais a paine puet estre amant sans jalousie, ne l'amante pareillement. /

201r 49. Beau Sire, je vous demande pourquoy amours [n']est ne* [ne] peut estre sans jalousie?
Dame, pour l'aspreté d'amours, et pour les mesdisans, et pour ce que les cuers ne les voulentez ne sont mye, ne ne peuent estre tousjours en ung estat ne en ung propoz sans varier.

50. Beau Sire, je vous demande se la jalousie est bonne en amours?
Dame, elle y est bonne et mauvaise: bonne pour ce que l'amant qui est jaloux met tousjours paine en luy tellement desguiser, ordonner, et maintenir, qu'il plaise myeulx a sa dame que nulz autres; et aussy bien vous dy je de l'amye comme de l'amy, sy que l'en devient plus saige et myeulx celant; et d'autrepart est jalousie tresmauvaise, en tant que nul ne nulle, puys qu'il scet et congnoist la bonté et la valeur de la personne qu'il ayme, ne doit estre jaloux ne jalouse. /

201v 51. Beau Si[r]e, je vous demande: l'amant qui est jaloux de s'amye, luy doit il nommer la personne dont la jalousie naist, ne l'amye a son amy?
Dame, nennil.
Raison pourquoy?
Pour ce que lui ou elle pourroit estre jaloux sans cause de jalousie; que se il ou elle le disoit, et fust a cause ou sans cause, il ou elle le pourroit bien mettre en voye de penser a celluy ou a celle dont il ou elle sy s'en mescroiroit, sy que ce est sottie du dire et nommer la personne dont elle vient. Et sachiez que nulle autre folie ne sotye je ne scay en jalousie.

52. Dame, je vous demande et prye par la force du jeu et du

*MS ou

royaulme ou nul ne nulle ne doit mentir, dittes moy verité, se les femmes sont aussi jalouses que hommes sont?

Beau Sire, je cuide que ouyl; et plus legierement doivent estre jalouses que les hommes, selon ce qu'il me semble, et verité est selon
202r / ce que j'espoir.

53. Dame, je vous demande pourquoy les femmes doivent estre plus tost jalouses que les hommes?

[Beau Sire], pour ce que les hommes vont en plusieurs lieux, et voyent tant d'unes et d'autres, que a paine se peuent leurs cuers tenir qu'ilz ne varient, et qu'ilz n'en pryent aucunes d'aymer.

54. Dame, je vous demande se la jalousie de la femme dure plus que celle de l'omme?

Beau Si[r]e, je croy que celle de l'omme est plus durant, en tant qu'il est vertueux plus que la femme ne soit.

55. Dame, je vous demande et pry a qui jalousie dure plus et griefve, que vous le me dittes, soit a l'omme ou a la femme?[33]

Beau Sire, elle griefve plus a la femme.

Raison pourquoy?

Pour ce que la femme est de plus fieble complexion que n'est
202v l'omme, si / que la voulenté ne doit mye si durant estre que celle
de l'omme. Mais elle dure plus en l'omme, comme j'ay dit; et de tant qu'elle dure moins en la femme que en l'omme, la* sent elle plus asprement, sy luy est plus griefve.

56. Dame, je vous demande, s'il estoit ainsy que ung homme ou une femme en leur jeune aage commençast a aymer a quinse ans et adonc laissast l'aymer, et ung homme ou une femme aussy en vieil aage commençast a aymer (a cincquante ans)[34] et adonc laissast l'aymer, et ung homme ou une femme commençast aussi a amer a cincquante ans et aymast jusques a la fin, je vous demande lequel feroit myeulx le sien devoir envers amours, et qui seroit plus vray amant?

Beau Sirc, cellui qui commence a aymer a cincquante ans et le maintenist jusques a la mort.

Raison pourquoy?

203r Pour ce que / celluy n'ayma oncques de parfaitte amour ne vraye

*MS: le

qu'il se repentist en nul temps ne fausist d'aymer. Et s'il avoit monstré aussy grant amour et semblant d'amer que oncques fist homme, et il se repentist en aucun temps, tous ses biens fais devroyent estre comptez pour neant. Et greigneur guerdon devroit avoir icelluy qui commenceroit a cincquante ans, et adonc mourust vray amant dedens le tiers jour, que celluy qui auroit aymé jusques a cincquante ans.

57. Dame, se j'avoye une femme que j'aymasse bien, je vous demande se je devroye avoir plus chier que elle amast avecques moy de vraye amour ung autre homme, et feusse bien certain qu'elle ne se meffist en nulle maniere, ne ja ne deust meffaire, et fust humble et debonnaire envers moy, ou qu'elle n'aymast ou fust rioteuse?

Beau Sire, vous devriez myeulx aymer qu'elle aymast. /

203v Raison pourquoy?

Pour ce qu'elle seroit tousjours joyeuse et en desir de vous servir a gré, et sy se soustendroit plus honnestement de cuer et de corps, et myeulx pourriez faire vostre voulenté.

58. Dame, il est une damoyselle que deux hommes requierent d'amours et l'ayment. Et avient qu'elle doit aller hors de la ville, sy emprunte le cheval de l'un et la housse et le chappel de l'autre; sy vous demande auquel elle est plus tenue, et lequel elle doit myeulx amer?

Beau Sire, celluy de qui elle emprunte la housse et le chappel, selon mon advis.

Raison pourquoy?

Sire, pour ce qu'elle ne le* puet plus honnourer que de porter et vestir son propre habit; et aussi ne puet luy estre plus honnouré, pour ce que bien luy appert qu'elle l'ayme myeulx, quant elle met le syen plus pres de son cuer, et en pare son corps.

204r 59. Dame, ung homme a amee une / femme et ayme, mais il ne puet trouver en elle pitié ne mercy, ainçoys luy escondit tousjours s'amour, et luy dit qu'il soit certain que ja ne l'aymera. Et une** aultre vient a luy et dit ainsy: Doulx amy, il me semble que celle que vous aymez sy ne vous ayme point, ains perdez vostre temps a elle aymer. Et je suys celle qui a le cuer tendre et espris de vostre amour, et grant voulenté ay de vous aymer. Et ce elle luy fiance de sa main.

*MS: se **MS: ung

Je vous demande s'il doit celle laisser ou il ne puet nulle mercy trouver, ou aymer celle qui luy offre s'amour?

Beau Sire, nennil.

Raison pourquoy?

Pour ce que fin cuer ne se doit retraire d'aymer pour nul escondit ne pour nul mal sentir; ains ait tousjours espoir que sa dame aura mercy de luy en aucun temps.

60. Dame, je vous demande, pour ce que femme apperçoit par
204v regart et par contenance que ung homme l'ayme, / savoir s'elle auroit plus chier qu'il luy deist ou* qu'il s'en deportast?

Beau Sire, je croy qu'elle aymeroit myeulx qu'il s'en souffrist du dire que ce qu'il lui deist; et en tant comme de moy, je l'aymeroye myeulx.

61. Dame, je vous demande qui ayme plus asprement, ou l'omme ou la femme?

[Beau Sire], la femme, sy comme je croy.

Raison pourquoy?

Pour ce que l'omme puet et doit dire tout hardyment a femme sa voulenté; et ce ne puet mye dire femme, sauve son honneur.

62. Beau Sire, je vous demande laquelle amour est plus durant, ou celle de l'omme, ou celle de la femme?

Dame, c'est celle de l'omme qui selon nature doit plus durer; mais les hommes sont si variables et sy divers orendroit que je croy que l'amour de la femme dure plus, et sy est ce contre le droit de nature.[35]

205r 63. Dame, je vous demande, se ung hom- / me avoit aymé de fin cuer une femme dix ans et n'eust trouvé en elle nul confort, s'il s'en pourroit et devroit partir selon raison et aymer une** autre?

Sire, nennyl.

Cause pourquoy?

Pour ce que vraye amour n'a point de fin, sy comme vous avez dit par devant, sy qu'il n'est nul amant vray qui pour longue attente se retrait d'aymer celle ou son cuer s'est mys.

*MS: que **MS: ung

64. Dame, trois hommes ayment une femme et bien le scevent, sy que ilz s'accordent tous ensemble d'aller parler a elle pour savoir auquel elle se voudra tenir; et a celluy la laisseront a qui elle s'accordera le myeulx. Et lui vont demander qu'elle leur dye. Elle, qui sage est et subtive, prent l'un par le doy et lui estraint, le second elle luy marche sur le pié, et au tiers elle guygne de l'ueil. Je vous demande lequel de ces trois hommes elle ayme le myeulx?

205v Sire, c'est / cellui a qui elle guygne de l'ueil, car tout ce que les yeux font naist du cuer, et plus soubtivement ne luy puet faire assavoir.[36]

65. Dame, je vous demande, se aucuns amant et amye avoyent par amours esté menez a ce que l'amy eust jeü avec l'amye, se l'en puet ou doit ce meffait pardonner par raison?

Beau Sire, nennyl.

Cause pourquoy?

Car le dit meffait est sy grant et tel que l'en n'en puet faire amendement, ne restaurer la perte, sy que on ne le puet ne doit pardonner. Neantmoins le puet bien et doit pitié excuser, mais raison ne le puet accorder.[37]

66. Dame, se l'en devoit maintenant passer mer pour aler en saincte terre, et il convenist a vostre amy, se vous l'aviez, aler avec les autres et la se marier a une* autre que a vous, et pour ce y demourroit, je vous demande se vous voudriez qu'il se mariast cy?

206r Beau Sire, / j'aymeroye myeulx qu'il alast oultre mer, car j'auroye espoir qu'il retournast et se amendast.

67. Dame, je vous demande dont souspir amoureux vient?

Beau Sire, de doulce pensee couverte en plaisant desir, nourry en espoir d'amours a ce que le cuer desire honnourablement.

68. Dame, je vous demande dont amoureux souspir vient, se souspir vient d'autre lieu?

Sire, ouyl.

Et Dame, dont vient il?

Sire, d'aucun ennuy que enuyeux et mesdisans font a amant et amye en plusieurs fais.

69. Dame, je vous demande de qui les souspirs sont plus grans, ou de l'omme, ou de la femme?

*MS: ung

Beau Sire, de la femme.

Raison pourquoy?

Pour ce qu'il luy grieve plus au cuer de ce qu'elle n'ose dire sa voulenté qu'il ne fait a l'amant, car de tant comme la femme est plus
206v tendre et de plus feble complexion / que l'omme n'est, dc tant luy griefve il plus au cuer.

70. Dame, je vous demande qui est de plus aspre voulenté d'aymer, ou l'omme ou la femme?

Beau Sire, la femme.

Dame, pourquoy?

Pour ce qu'il avient que la femme cele et coeuvre sa voulenté a son desir pour la doubtance de son honneur amenrir, dont elle est aucuneffois blecee au cuer.

71. Dame, je vous demande se femme puet avoir deux amys?

Beau Sire, nennyl, neant plus qu'elle puet partir son cuer en deux partyes.

72. Dame, je vous demande, se il estoit ainsy que ung homme aymast une femme de si hault lieu et sy riche qu'elle ne luy appartenist mye a aymer, et qu'il ne luy osast dire son estat, comment le luy pourroit il faire savoir et en plus belle maniere?

Beau Sire, par la regarder piteusement. /

207r 73. Dame, je vous demande se par elle regarder l'amant pourroit dame ou damoyselle esmouvoir a ce qu'elle eust pitié et mercy de luy, sy qu'elle l'aymast?

Beau Sire, ouyl; de telle condicion pourroit la femme estre par nature. Neantmoins se doit la femme doubter que l'omme ne soit acoustumé de regarder ainsy, et pour ce l'amour de regart n'est mye sceüre.

74. Dame, je vous demande comment homme puet myeulx et plus tost avenir a l'amour de femme?

Beau Sire, par grace, dont mercy naist.

75. Dame, je vous demande comment amant puet avoir grace d'estre aymé de s'amye?

Beau Sire, par estre courtoys, loyal, certain, franc, secret, symple, attempré, et celant. Tel doit loyal amant estre.

76. Dame, il sont deux damoiselles manans en ung hostel, belles
207v et gracieuses, dont l'une a eu ung homme par / long temps chier, et encores a; mais il ne l'ayme point, ainz ayme l'autre de tout son cuer, et elle ne l'ayme pas. Je vous demande s'il esloingnera celle qu'il ayme et qui ne l'ayme point, et aymera celle qui l'a aymé long temps, et encores ayme?

Beau Sire, il ne puet ne ne doit esloingner au droit d'amours et selon le droit des amans celle qu'il ayme. Il convient qu'il ne l'ayme pas.

77. Dame, il est ung homme qui a aymé belle, mais long temps l'a eslongié et ne luy a mye pleu. Or avient d'aventure qu'il ayme de rechief celle mesmes; et elle, quant elle voit ce, luy monstre grant semblant de hayr, pour ce qu'elle en a aymé ung autre, et par despit de la deffaulte de luy. Je vous demande qu'il fera, ou de plus avant aler, ou la* laisser?

Beau Sire, il ne la doit mye laissier, ains luy doit offrir cuer et corps, et luy dire que ce qui l'avoit eslongié, ce fut par folour, et
208r qu'il s'en repent; et luy prye qu'elle luy pardoinst, / ainsy pourra avoir pitié de luy tant qu'elle l'aymera.

78. Dame, il est ung homme qui a une femme espousee, belle et gracieuse, de qui il est chier tenu et bien aymé, et il en ayme une aultre layde, nyce, et sauvaige, de tout son cuer. Je vous demande par quelle raison il laisse sa belle, doulce amye, pour aymer la layde et mesprisee?

Beau Sire, je vous dy que c'est folye et rage qui a ce l'esmeult par son vollage cuer, car pis ne puet il faire que de laisser sa certaine amye, qui est belle et gracieuse, pour en aymer une layde et sauvaige. Neantmoins il ne est nulle layde amye ne nul lait amy [qu']amours [ne] les fait tous et toutes sembler belles.

79. Dame, je vous demande lequel valt myeulx a fin amant pour lui faire valoir et pour luy [faire][38] vivre au mains de bataille et d'ennuy, ou qu'il faille a recevoir l'amour de son amye pour doubte
208v d'estre / apperçu, ou qu'il en jouysse et que plusieurs l'apperçoivent, sy que elle en soit blasmee et amenrie de son honneur, et a grant meschief de cuer?

*MS: le

Beau Sire, il vaut myeulx qu'il y faille.

Raison pourquoy?

Pour ce que celluy n'est mye amant qui tant a avoir l'amour de s'amye en maniere qu'elle en puisse estre ou soit blasmee ne empiree, sy qu'il vault myeulx a souffrir.

80. Dame, lequel aymeriez vous myeulx, ou avoir ou savoir?

Beau Sire, j'aymeroye myeulx a savoir que a avoir.

Raison pourquoy?

Pour ce que se j'estoye garnye de savoir, j'auroye encore assez d'avoir.[39]

81. Dame, je vous demande lequel vault myeulx a dame ou a damoyselle qui aymer veult honnourablement pour honneur ou pour myeulx valoir, ou a donner ou a (ap)prendre?

Beau Sire, l'un et l'autre n'est bon, ne n'affiert a elle.* Mais toutesvoyes, se faire le couvient, plus belle chose est de donner a elle que de prendre.

209r Raison pour- / quoy?

Pour ce que femme qui prent, elle se vent, et est tenu[e] de rendre. Et s'elle donne, cellui a qui le don est fait l'en doit myeulx aymer, honnourer, et servir sans penser a nulle mauvaistié, car celluy n'est mye amy qui** pense a nulle vilennye.

82. Dame, je vous requier et prye moult amyablement par la force du jeu et par la foy que vous devez au Roy qui ne ment, que vous me vueillez dire quelle est la mendre[40] tache et la plus belle que vray amy puist avoir, et qui myeulx doit plaire a s'amye?

Beau Sire, c'est qu'il soit en tous fais courtois, symple, et bien celant.

83. Dame, je vous demande se prouesse et hardement esmeuvent point le cuer de dame a aymer?

Beau Sire, ouyl, car femme de sa nature desire tousjours que celluy qu'elle entent a aymer soit hardy et preux.

Dame, pourquoy?

Pour ce qu'elle en est plus honnouree, et plus creue,[41] et myeulx prisiee; et ce desire cuer de femme. /

*MS: luy **MS: qiy

209v 84. Dame, je vous demande quel est le mantel d'amours sans penne?

(Beau Sire, ouyl, car femme de sa nature desire tousjours que celluy qu'elle entent a aymer soit hardy et preux.

Dame, pourquoy?

Pour ce qu'elle en est plus honnouree)

Beau Sire, le mantel d'amours, c'est une nyce demande; et non pourtant je vous diray ce que j'en scay: aucuns dyent que c'est acoler sans baisier.

85. Dame, je vous demande qu'est honneur?

Beau Sire, soy maintenir sy bien, sy saigement, et sy ordonneement que chascun en dye bien, et estre large et despendre largement qui a de quoy; et qui n'a de quoy, si ait bonne voulenté.

86. Dame, je vous demande que est dit largesse?

Beau Sire, donner largement et habondamment, faire festes, et donner a mengier souvent.

87. Dame, je vous demande qu'est courtoysie?

210r Beau Sire, c'est estre doulx et a- / myable de parolles, et donner voulentiers beaulx dons, car courtoysie vient de largesse.

88. Dame, je vous demande lequel vous auriez plus chier, ou que vostre amy, se vous l'avez ou attendez a avoir, fust large, courtoys, et couars, ou eschars, avaricieux, et hardy?

Beau Sire, j'aymeroye trop qu'il fust saige, large, courtoys, et couars, car hardement ne puet longtemps demourer en cuer avaricieux et eschars; car avarice, qui est ung pechié mortel, ne le laisse jamais en paix. Et certaine suy que Dieu ayme trop mieulx saige couardyse que fol hardement; et aussi font tous bons cuers.

Cy finissent les Demandes d'Amours

NOTES TO THE TEXTS

All references in these notes to the *De Amore* are taken from the Walsh edition (see Introduction, notes 15 and 16); for details of Klein's work on the *Demandes d'Amour*, see Introduction, note 22.

[1] The details concerning Abelard which are alluded to in this opening paragraph stem from his autobiographical *Historia Calamitatum*, except that his reason for establishing the Paraclete in the first place was to escape persecution, however much in other respects 'sa conscience le reprist'. He first set himself up there in the early 1120s, building a simple mud and wattle oratory, but students came from Paris to be with him, and helped build a larger and more solid oratory. He himself left the Paraclete in 1125 or 1126 to become Abbot of St Gildas de Rhuys in Brittany, but in 1129 he settled Heloise and her nuns there, after they had been expelled from the Convent at Argenteuil by Abbot Suger of St Denis.

As for the details concerning Heloise, the title 'abbesse' is probably taken from the *Roman de la Rose* (vv. 8730–31, 8775, and 8786 in the Lecoy edition, *CFMA*), though it was also used during her lifetime. As for her learning, Abelard attests to it in the *Historia Calamitatum*, while Peter the Venerable, writing to Heloise after Abelard's death in 1142, offers the following recollection in praise of her: 'I had yet not quite passed the bounds of youth and reached early manhood when I knew of your name and your reputation, not yet for religion but for your virtuous and praiseworthy studies. I used to hear at that time of the woman who although still caught up in the obligations of the world, devoted all her application to knowledge of letters, something which is very rare, and to the pursuit of secular learning, and that not even the pleasures of the world, with its frivolities and delights, could distract her from this worthy determination to study the arts' (*The Letters of Abelard and Heloise*, translated by Betty Radice [Harmondsworth: Penguin, 1974] p. 277). Jean de Meun, too, in the *Roman de la Rose*, refers to her as 'bien antendanz et bien letree' (v. 8735; see also vv. 8743–44 and 8797). The precise details claimed here of her attitudes are fanciful, but the statement that 'elle hayoit luxure' could be based on the fact that in her letters to Abelard she was careful always to draw a distinction between love and lust. In her first letter she half-accuses Abelard of mere lust, not love, when she complains that he had abandoned her after their mutual entry into religious life; and in her second letter she refers to his castration as a punishment suited only to adulterers. Her unswerving devotion to Abelard through all vicissitudes and her cruel plight would be a sufficient basis on which to build for her a reputation that would fit her for the teaching task assigned to her in this paragraph.

[2] The range of imagery to describe love which is reflected in this treatise is examined in my article 'Un *Art d'Amour* inédit de la fin du moyen âge: son cadre et ses métaphores' (see Introduction, note 9).

[3] For a general table of comparable passages in this *Art d'Amour* and the *De Amore*, see Introduction, pp. 11–12.

[4] Andreas (I, 5 §§2–3) gives 50 as the upper age limit for a woman's interest in love.

[5] This point is in fact never taken up in the *Art d'Amour*, because it is based on the statement in Andreas that 'love burns in a woman at an earlier age than among men' (I, 5 §5), and the reference is to a section of text beyond the end of the French treatise (see Walsh, p. 41, note 20[a]).

[6] 'donne' is probably an error for 'denie'.

[7] Compare the four stages which Andreas gives (I, 6 §60): 'The first stage lies in allowing the suitor hope, the second in granting a kiss, the third in the enjoyment of an embrace, and the fourth is consummated in the yielding of the whole person' (Walsh, p. 57).

[8] This is the first of five passages in which bird-imagery is used to describe the love-relationships between various social groups (see below notes 11, 13, 16 and 22). Nobility and boldness are here represented by the falcon and goshawk ('austour'), aristocratic male birds for whom the partridge and pheasant are legitimate prey. The kite ('escouffle') represents those who, by their social rank and their general character, are less worthy of such prey. In *L'Escoufle* by Jean Renart, the crisis in the story occurs when a kite seizes Aelis's purse and flies off with it, thinking it to be a piece of meat. In the Introduction to his edition of the romance (*TLF*, Geneva, Droz, 1974) Franklin Sweetser comments that 'cet oiseau était évidemment un objet de mépris au moyen âge' (p. xxx). Later in the romance, when Guillaume captures a kite, he tears it apart in a fit of rage and eats the heart raw (vv. 6898–6903). Compare also *King Lear*, I, 4, when Lear says to the Duke of Albany: 'Detested kite, thou liest'. The contempt felt towards this bird may well have its origins in the fact that much of the kite's food consists of carrion rather than prey.

[9] The addition of the formula concerning Heloise and her pupil renders this sentence meaningless. It corresponds in the *De Amore* to the closing sentence of a speech by the noblewoman to the commoner: 'So my argument makes it clear that your efforts are superfluous, and you will later realise that your toil has been to no purpose' (Walsh, I, 6 § 88, p. 65).

[10] This passage, from 'Tout amant ...' (f. 154[v]), is discussed in the Introduction, pp. 14–15.

[11] Although it is of the same family as the falcon, the 'faucon lasnier' (lanner) is, like the kite in note 8 above, a less worthy creature, which sometimes succeeds in capturing prey to which it should not be entitled, while the humble sparrow can sometimes chase away a kestrel ('mouchet').

[12] This is no more than part of the rendering of 'antiquitus' ('in ancient times')

in Andreas (I, 6 §107). At the bottom of f. 165r the same word is rendered simply as 'anciennement'.

[13] Just as in note 11 above a sparrow can sometimes chase away a kestrel, so a kestrel can on occasion chase away a falcon; a lanner (inferior falcon) is sometimes equated with a kestrel. The point is clearer in Andreas: 'it is true that a falcon is sometimes routed by a kestrel, yet that falcon is numbered amongst falcons but the kestrel amongst kestrels, with the reservation that the first will be called a poor falcon, the second a very good kestrel' (Walsh, I, 6 §110, p. 71). There is therefore a range of 'nobility' and worth in each social stratum.

[14] This passage, beginning 'Et pour ce que l'amante ne veult pas reprendre ...' (f. 160r) is discussed in the Introduction, p. 15.

[15] Interestingly, Andreas has said 'comitissa vel marchionissa' ('countess or marchioness') (Walsh, I, 6 §119, p. 74); etymologically 'marquis(e)' is derived from 'marche' ('frontier').

[16] If, through exceptional ferocity, an unworthy and socially inferior bird succeeds in capturing a partridge (cf. notes 8, 11 and 13 above), he would not be able to keep her for long.

[17] This passage, from 'L'abbesse Heloys demonstre et enseigne a son disciple comment ...' (f. 164v) is discussed in the Introduction, p. 13.

[18] This passage, from 'Et par ceste raison ...' (f. 167r) is discussed in the Introduction, p. 14; 'es parties de France' corresponds in Andreas to 'in Italiae finibus'! See Walsh (p. 80, n. 61) for the possible identity of the count to whom Andreas was referring.

[19] According to Walsh (p. 80, n. 62) the contemporary King of Hungary, Bela III, was actually tall and handsome.

[20] Ecclesiasticus, 21.23 (Walsh). The corresponding verse in the A.V. is 20.

[21] The French text here rather confuses the clear distinction made in Andreas, who states (I, 6 §§167–68) that only a man of higher rank can sit by a woman without first asking permission; a man of similar rank should ask permission, while a man of lower rank cannot ask it, but she may invite him, as the French text goes on to state.

[22] The original sense of Andreas's text, as translated by Walsh, was: 'A pheasant captured by a sparrowhawk is thought more worth having than one caught by a large hawk' (p. 89). In a note (p. 88) he explains that here the pheasant signifies worth of character, the sparrowhawk is a common woman, and the large hawk is a noblewoman. In the French text the sense is merely that the object of love captured by a nobleman is more esteemed than that of lesser birds.

[23] All that appears to be missing at this point is the completion of the sentence, which corresponds to the closing sentence of Dialogue D in Andreas, the end of the discussion between the nobleman and the common woman: 'Though I shall it seems leave you in body, I remain closely bound to you in heart' (Walsh, p. 97). The next sentence marks the start of Dialogue E.

[24] Again, the equivalent of the end of a sentence is missing: 'Though in time

of heat the life of crops may be prolonged by light showers, they cannot avoid the danger of drought unless they are soaked in torrents of rain' (Walsh, I, 6, §206, p. 99).

[25] The *Art d'Amour* ends with the two allegories of the future life, found in the *De Amore*, I, 6, §222–273. In Andreas there is in both of them a graphic account of the rewards and punishments given to women according to their attitude and response to love during their lifetime. Both are incomplete in the French treatise. This description of the 'pallais d'amour' represents only the beginning of the first of the allegories. Because it ends abruptly we are never told the significance of the four doorways. In Andreas the eastern entrance is reserved for the god of love ('deus', not 'royne d'amours'); the one facing south is for those ladies who linger on the threshold and give their love to men who prove worthy after careful scrutiny and enquiry; the door to the west is frequented by prostitutes, who give themselves indiscriminately to all men; and those who guard the northern entrance are women who resolutely refuse entry to the palace to all men, though they are themselves loved and courted by men. In response to this explanation by the nobleman, the noblewoman claims to belong safely to the group of women at the northern entrance, to which the man replies: 'Then hear the endless punishment awaiting you' (§229).

This resolve provides the man with the opportunity to relate the story of the visit to the 'verger d'amour' and the meeting with the god of love. Again, in the French treatise the story is mutilated and reduced. It begins in Walsh at §229, but the start in the *Art d'Amour* ('L'abesse Heloys demonstre au sien disciple que une dame estoit ...') corresponds to §237. Because of this omission and others within the episode the reader is deprived of background information on the three groups of women riding to meet the god of love to receive their just deserts. Nevertheless the text does make clear that 'ce dieu sy donne a chascun amant guerdon selon ce qu'il a desservy' (f. 184^{v}), though it does not preserve a complete description of the various areas allotted to the different groups of women (see Introduction, pp. 12–13). The lady riding the scraggy horse was among those who refused love, and so was destined for punishment, but the messenger succeeds in the *De Amore* in pleading for a reduced sentence from the god of love. As for the presence of the messenger in the story, the Latin treatise makes it clear that he had fallen asleep and lost his way while seeking his master, and came upon the vision related. His privilege is to meet the god of love and to tell the world all that he has seen and been told.

[26] Apart from the omission of the messenger's plea on behalf of the lady who had introduced him to the 'verger', the French text here omits the twelve precepts of love delivered by the god (§§268–69).

[27] The meaning of this line as it stands is not clear. The other published MSS which contain this question have only the first line, but the Wolfenbüttel MS has: 'Qui est la chambre ou sont les lits / Et toute joie et tous *delits*?' (f. 19b), and the Chantilly MS: 'Quelle est la chambre ou son lit / Est et toute joye et tout *delit*?'

(f. 42c). One of the printed versions published by Klein has: 'Qui est la chambre, ou est le lit / Et toute joye et tout *deduit*?' (*Les Adevineaux Amoureux*, II, 7; Klein, p. 179), and in another the question is in prose: 'Le nom de la chambre ou les lieux sont de toutes joyes et de *delitz*' (*Les Demandes d'Amours*, 16; Klein, p. 163). In *Le Chevalier Errant*, too, a similar question occurs in prose: 'Amie, quelle est la chambre ou sont les liz ou on a le *premier delit* d'amours?' (Finoli, art. cit., p. 262; see Introduction, note 41 for details of this article).

[28] All the other versions published by Klein, together with the Chantilly and Wolfenbüttel MSS, have 'haut' in this line in place of 'vault': 'Aux fins amanz qui ament *aut*' (B.N. fr. 12615, No. 16; Klein, p. 145); 'Amis, amans qui aimme *haut*' (Montpellier, Fac. Méd. 236, No. 10; Klein, p. 151); 'Aux vrays amans qui aiment *hault*' (*Les Adevineaux Amoureux*, I, 2; Klein, pp. 175–76); 'Aux fins amans qui ayment *hault*' (*Demandes et Responces d'Amours*, No. 5; Klein, p. 169). Klein corrects the reading of MS 16 F II to 'Amie, amant qui ayment hault' (p. 158), with no acknowledgement that the MS has 'vault'. As it stands the MS reading can only mean: 'Dearest, a lover, who wishes to love' (i.e. declare his love).

[29] This concept seems to derive from the *Roman de la Rose*.

[30] The situation is clearer in one of the printed versions of this question published by Klein: 'Or est le cas tel qu'il leur fault passer une riviere. Mais la fortune est qu'il convient l'une d'elles noyer. Et en vous est de rescourre et sauver, laquele qu'il vous plaist ...' (*Les Adevineaux Amoureux*, I, 30; Klein, p. 115).

[31] Compare the reading of B.N. fr. 757: '...quelle est la cortoisie qi puet estre en amors sanz penser, sanz desir, sanz espoir, et sanz joir?' (Klein, II, 7; p. 71).

[32] Compare the reading of the Chantilly MS: 'Sire, je vous demande se les mesdisans savoient l'amour des vraiz amans, se il ne leur pourroit par nulle maniere en riens prouffiter?' (f. 24b).

[33] In the Chantilly MS this question is split into two separate but adjacent questions: 'Sire, je vous demande auquel jalousie dure plus longuement, ou a l'omme ou a la femme?' (the answer is different from P.55), and 'Sire, je vous demande a qui jalousie griefve plus, ou a l'homme ou a la femme?' (Answer: 'a la femme') (f. 21d).

[34] The deleted phrase 'a cincquante ans' probably belongs in the preceding line after 'et adonc laissast l'aymer'. In all other MSS containing this question there are only two instances cited to choose from: a young couple who love from the age of 15 (or 16) to 50, and another couple from 50 to the end of their lives. The question in MS 16 F II should probably also have only the two, as no reference is made in the answer to the elderly couple.

[35] Klein changes 'Beau Sire' to 'Dame' and vice-versa in this question, pointing out in a footnote (p. 56) that all other versions which have an equivalent question address it to the 'Dame'.

[36] This question is more precisely worded in *Les Adevineaux Amoureux*, I, 22, since it asks: 'auquel elle donne plus grant signe d'amour?'; to which the answer

is: 'Damoiselle, [a] cellui a qui elle gingne, car l'ueil c'est le messagier du cuer et non le doy ne le pied' (Klein, p. 113).

[37] This question seems strangely harsh and puritanical, at odds with the general spirit of the collection. Its equivalent is not found in any of the other MSS, or in any of the printed versions published by Klein. Is it purely coincidental that this question, which sets limits to amorous dalliance, appears in a MS compiled for the young prince? There is no evidence or suggestion of eclecticism in the collection of *Demandes d'Amour* in MS 16 F II.

[38] An alternative emendation would be simply to delete 'luy' and read 'pour vivre', as in other versions published by Klein.

[39] This question, which apparently has nothing to do directly with love, is also found virtually identically in B.N. fr. 1130 (II, 11; Klein, p. 89). When it occurs in one of the printed editions (*Les Demandes d'Amours*), the answer is given as: 'J'aymeroye mieulx sçavoir, car pour sçavoir on acquiert moult de bien et d'onneur' (I, 15; Klein, p. 137).

[40] Klein (p. 62), following the other MSS which have the equivalent question, corrects 'mendre' to 'meilleur'. The reading in the Chantilly MS for this question is 'la mendre chose et la plus belle ...' (f. 39d).

[41] Both Chantilly (f. 40a) and Wolfenbüttel (f. 18a) read 'cremue' for 'creue'.

GLOSSARY

The glossary is selective. Normally only the first occurrence of a particular word or form is listed, unless there is a difference of meaning. Reference is given to the folio (r or v) in the case of words glossed in the *Art d'Amour*; for the *Demandes d'Amour* reference is made to the verse or prose question (V.1, V.2, etc., or P.1, P.2, etc.) in which the word is to be found.

accointement, s.m.; accointemens, 144^r, familiarity.
accroissance, s.f., P.40, increase.
admonnestement, s.m., 148^v, prompting.
admonnester, v; admonneste, pres. ind. 3, 148^v, prompt.
aherdre, v. refl.; ahert, pres. ind. 3, 176^r; aherdent, pres. ind. 6, 140^r, cling to.
amaison, s.m., 144^v, hook.
apparoir, v. 145^v, appear.
araisonnement, s.m., 158^r, speech.
ardoir, v.n.; art, pres. ind. 3, P.9; ardent, pres. ind. 6, 143^v, burn.
arraisonner, v.a.; arraisonnees, p.p., 155^r, address.
attemperance, s.f., 143^r; attrempance, V.3, moderation.
attempreement, adv., 170^v, with moderation.
attemprer, v.a.; attempré, P.1, attrempez, P.22, attrempee, P.23, p.p. and adj., moderate, temperate.
attouchement, s.m.; attouchemens, 137^v, contact.
attrempance, v. attemperance.
attrempez, attrempee, v. attemprer.
avecques, prep. P.57, in addition to.
avision, s.f., 181^r, vision.
baillier, v; baillees, p.p., 166^v, organized, delivered.
bouter (hors), v; bouté, P.7, boutez, 159^r, p.p., expel.
carnel, s.m.; carneaulx, V.3, crenels.
charniere, s.f., 183^v, lit. hinge; doorway.
cognard, adj., 140^v, stupid.
command, s.m., 157^r, commandment.
concevement, s.m.; concevemens, 180^r, conception, inspiration.
contenement, s.m., 140^r, disposition, countenance; contenemens, 137^r, conduct.
controuveur, s.m.; controuveurs, 171^r, inventor.
coquart, s.m.; coquars, 156^v, fop.
corrompance, s.f., 170^v, corruption.
cremeur, s.f., P.19, fear.
cure, s.f., 172^r, care.
curiable, adj.; curiables, 171^v, hospitable.
deité, s.f., 148^v, ?
delectableté, s.f., 184^v, delight, joy.

demonstrement, s.m.; demonstremens, 182^{v}, display.
departement, s.m., 182^{r}, departure.
deporter, v. refl.; deportast, imp. subj. 3, P.60, refrain.
descouvenable, adj.; descouvenables, 164^{r}, inappropriate, unseemly.
descouvrir, v.a., P.45, reveal.
despisier, v.a.; despise, pres. subj. 3, 167^{v}, despise.
dilacion, s.f., 178^{v}, delay.
doubtance, s.f., P.70, fear.
elusable, adj.; elusables, 148^{r}, deceiving, insincere.
entablement, s.m., 138^{v}, support.
entalentement, s.m., 168^{r}; entalentemens, 153^{r}, desire, wish.
ententif, adj., P.26, intent (upon).
entre-arraisnier, v. refl; arresnent, pres. ind. 6, 170^{v}, communicate, talk to one another.
entrelaissement, s.m., 169^{r}, respite.
escondire, v.a.; escondit, pres. ind. 3, P.5, refuse.
escondit, s.m., P.20, refusal.
escouffle, s.m. or f., 153^{v}, kite.
esleessier, v.a.; esleesse, pres. ind. 3, 156^{r}, rejoice.
estrangier, v.a.; estrangez, p.p., 158^{v}, remove, banish.
exemple, s.f., 175^{r}, illustration.
faucon lasnier, v. lasnier.
foloyer, v.n., 147^{r}, act foolishly.
forsenerie, s.f., 152^{v}, frenzy.
franchise, s.f., 143^{v}, freedom.
frire, v.n.; frit, pres. ind. 3, P.9, burn (with longing, desire).
fuzel, s.m., 153^{v}, spindle.
gergonnement, s.m., 174^{r}, chirping.
gest, s.m.; en gest, 142^{r}, on heat?
glay, s.m., P.25, tumult.
greigneur, adj., 152^{v}, greater.
hanter, v.a., 170^{v}, frequent.
housse, s.f., P.58, boot.
huan, s.m., 174^{v}, screech-owl, owl, or kite.
jangleur, s.m.; jangleurs, 171^{r}, gossip.
juxte, prep., 173^{r}, beside.
lasnier, adj., cowardly; faucon lasnier, s.m., 157^{r}, lanner.
leesse, s.f., P.5, joy.
lit, s.m., V.6 (line 2), ? See note to text.
los, v. loz.
loz, s.m., 151^{v}; los, P.6, reputation.
lyement, adv., V.7, joyously.
mauvaistié, s.f., P.81, wickedness.
meschief, s.m., P.79, misfortune, unhappiness.
mesparler, v., V.19, speak inappriopriately.
mierre, s.f., 185^{v}, myrrh.
mouchet, s.m., 157^{v}, small hawk or kestrel.

muement, s.m., 147^{r}, variation.
multipliance, s.f., P.40, abundance, increase.
nacion, s.f., 157^{v}, birth.
non-franc, adj. and s.m.; non-francs, 156^{v}, ignoble, unworthy.
non-noble, adj. and s.f., 176^{v}, one who is not noble in rank, commoner.
nyc, s.m., 167^{r}, nest.
nycetė, s.f., 171^{r}, naïvety.
onnyment, adv., 153^{v}, equally.
ordonnance, s.f., 185^{v}, arrangement.
ordonneement, adv., P.85, in orderly fashion.
outrecuidier, v.n.; oultrecuidiez, p.p. and adj., 156^{v}, presumptuous.
ouye, s.f.; ouyes, 137^{v}, act of hearing, listening.
pardurablement, adv., P.41, eternally.
passerel, s.m., 157^{v}, sparrow.
penne, s.f., P.84, lining, fur.
perfection, s.f., 143^{v}, achievement.
piteusement, adv., P.72, in a manner inspiring pity.
plaisance, s.f., P.1, pleasure.
poix, s.m., 149^{v}, what is (to be) weighed.
pourpenser, v.a.; pourpensoit, imp. ind. 3, 149^{v}, consider, reflect on.
proposement, s.m.; proposemens, 180^{r}, proposition.
quant, adj.; quantes, P.38, how many.
raiz, s.f., 142^{r}, snare.
rapine, s.f., 137^{v}, rapacity, theft.
ravoyer, v.a., P.21, restore to the right path.
respondre, v.a., 139^{v}, conceal.
retenue, s.f., 138^{r}, persistence.
reveleux, adj., P.25, boisterous.
rioteux, adj.; rioteuse, P.57, quarrelsome.
sayette, s.f., 151^{v}, arrow.
sottye, s.f., P.47; sotye, P.51, sottie, P.51, foolishness.
soubztraire, v.a.; soubztrayent, pres. subj. 6, 138^{v}, remove.
souffrete, s.f., 151^{v}, penury.
sourdre, v.n., 158^{v}, spring.
soustenement, s.m., 161^{r}, sustenance.
trespacement, s.m., 147^{r}, eager excess?
trespensyf, adj., P.26, preoccupied, deep in thought.
vault, V.16 (line 1), form of voloir, pres. ind. 3?
vertu, s.f., P.30, force, quality.
vertueux, adj., P.54, strong.
voyement, s.m.; voyemens, 137^{v}, act of seeing, perceiving.

APPENDIX

Alexander Klein, *Die altfranzösischen Minnefragen*, Marburger Beiträge zur romanischen Philologie, hg. von Ed. Wechssler, Heft I (Marburg: Adolf Ebel, 1911), consists of an edition and study of the love questions and answers contained in nine MSS of the fourteenth and fifteenth centuries, and three early printed versions of the late fifteenth or early sixteenth centuries. The table below is based principally on that published by Klein (pp. 19–28), and indicates the occurrence of comparable, but not necessarily completely identical, questions and answers in all known MSS. It includes two fifteenth-century MSS which did not figure in Klein's edition or table: Chantilly, Musée Condé 654 (formerly 1562) – the text of which is printed in James W. Hassell, *Amorous Games: a critical edition of 'Les Adevineaux amoureux'* (Austin: University of Texas, 1974) – and Wolfenbüttel, Herzog August Bibl. Guelf. 84.7.Aug.2. Their omission from Klein, along with that of several other early printed editions, was pointed out very soon after the appearance of Klein's work by Walther Suchier, 'Zu den altfranzösischen Minnefragen', *Zeitschrift für romanische Philologie*, 36 (1912), 221–28 (see also Eero Ilvonen's review of Klein in *Neuphilologische Mitteilungen*, 14 (1912), 218). Both MSS clearly derive from a common source, since all 70 prose and 29 verse questions relating to love in the Wolfenbüttel MS also occur in Chantilly in the same order (with one exception); but the Chantilly MS has over 200 prose and 31 verse questions on love, the extra prose ones being mostly interspersed between those which occur in both MSS. After a while both MSS, with no indication of the change, abandon love questions in favour of other types, including, with answers, mathematical conundrums and general riddles which, to begin with, are of almost a Christmas-cracker nature, but their merriment eventually comes to rely on elementary scatological or uninhibited sexual humour. The Chantilly MS returns at the end to a few, briefly-worded love questions. The riddles of the Wolfenbüttel MS, but not the love questions, are to be found in Bruno Roy, *Devinettes françaises du moyen âge* (Montréal–Paris: Bellarmin–Vrin, 1977).

Apart from the omission of these two important MSS, the Klein edition has other shortcomings. His transcription of the text of MS 16 F II is not very reliable, and this naturally undermines the reader's confidence in the accuracy of his transcription of the other MSS. Also the sigla he chose to designate the MSS are unnecessarily complex, in that he used one siglum to denote verse questions, and a different one for prose questions, if both occur in the same MS. His designations have been simplified as under; the MS which Klein knew as Cheltenham, Phillipps 8336 is now British Library Additional 46919, while the Westminster Abbey MS, which he referred to merely under the title 'Poésies françaises', is given its correct number:

		Klein
British Library, Royal 16 F II	La	M & A
British Library, Additional 46919	Lb	I
Bibliothèque Nationale, fr. 757	Pa	B
Bibliothèque Nationale, fr. 1130	Pb	C
Bibliothèque Nationale, fr. 12615	Pc	H
Bibliothèque de l'Arsenal, 5203 (copy of Berne, 218)	A	L
Oxford, Bodleian, MS Douce 308	O	D
Montpellier, Fac. Med. 236	M	K
Westminster Abbey 21	W	N & E
Chantilly, Musée Condé 654	C	-
Wolfenbüttel, Herzog August 84.7.Aug.2	Wo	-

The initial 'P' or 'V' alongside the cross in the table below indicates that a question has been transformed from verse to prose or vice-versa. The table is followed by an indication of those questions in MS 16 F II (La) which also occur in the three early printed editions used by Klein (Suchier, 222–25, listed a further 18 editions of the *Demandes*). Clearly Klein was able to examine only a small fraction of the editions which are extant, and a detailed study of all of them, though desirable, would be a considerable undertaking.

La	Lb	Pa	Pb	Pc	A	O	M	W	C	Wo	
V1	+			+	+		+	+	+	+	(V1)
V2	+			+	+		+	+	+	+	(V2)
V3	+			+	+		+		+	+	(V3)
V4	+			+	+		+	+	+	+	(V4)
V5	+			+	+		+	+	+	+	(V5)
V6					+P			+	+	+	(V6)
V7	+			+	+			+	+	+	(V7)
V8							+				(V8)
V9							+		+	+	(V9)
V10				+			+		+	+	(V10)
V11	+			+	+		+		+	+	(V11)
V12	+			+	+			+	+	+	(V12)

	La	Lb	Pa	Pb	Pc	A	O	M	W	C	Wo	
V13					+			+		+	+	(V13)
V14		+			+	+		+	+	+	+	(V14)
V15					+			+		+	+	(V15)
V16					+	+		+	+	+	+	(V16)
V17		+			+	+		+	+	+	+	(V17)
V18		+			+	+		+	+	+	+	(V18)
P1										+	+	(P1)
P2			+									(P2)
P3			+							+	+	(P3)
P4			+							+		(P4)
P5										+		(P5)
P6			+	+						+	+	(P6)
P7			+	+						+	+	(P7)
P8			+	+						+		(P8)
P9				+						+		(P9)
P10				+						+	+	(P10)
P11				+						+	+	(P11)
P12				+						+	+	(P12)
P13			+									(P13)
P14			+	+								(P14)
P15												(P15)
P16			+	+						+	+	(P16)
P17			+	+						+	+	(P17)
P18				+						+	+	(P18)
P19			+	+						+	+	(P19)
P20			+	+								(P20)
P21												(P21)
P22			+							+		(P22)
P23			+	+						+		(P23)
P24			+	+						+	+	(P24)
P25				+						+		(P25)
P26				+						+	+	(P26)
P27				+						+	+	(P27)
P28			+	+						+		(P28)
P29										+		(P29)
P30										+		(P30)
P31			+	+						+		(P31)
P32				+						+		(P32)
P33			+									(P33)
P34			+									(P34)

La	Lb	Pa	Pb	Pc	A	O	M	W	C	Wo	
P35			+						+		(P35)
P36			+								(P36)
P37		+	+						+	+	(P37)
P38									+	+	(P38)
P39									+	+	(P39)
P40									+	+	(P40)
P41		+							+	+	(P41)
P42		+									(P42)
P43		+							+		(P43)
P44											(P44)
P45		+	+						+		(P45)
P46			+								(P46)
P47									+	+	(P47)
P48											(P48)
P49											(P49)
P50									+	+	(P50)
P51			+								(P51)
P52		+	+					+			(P52)
P53			+								(P53)
P54		+	+								(P54)
P55		+	+					+	+	+	(P55)
P56		+	+			+		+	+		(P56)
P57		+	+								(P57)
P58			+						+		(P58)
P59							+				(P59)
P60		+							+		(P60)
P61											(P61)
P62		+						+			(P62)
P63		+									(P63)
P64		+							+	+	(P64)
P65									+	+	(P65)
P66						+			+		(P66)
P67		+						+			(P67)
P68											(P68)
P69		+						+			(P69)
P70		+						+	+		(P70)
P71									+	+	(P71)
P72		+									(P72)
P73		+									(P73)
P74		+	+								(P74)

La	Lb	Pa	Pb	Pc	A	O	M	W	C	Wo	
P75		+							+		(P75)
P76									+		(P76)
P77			+						+		(P77)
P78											(P78)
P79		+	+			+			+	+	(P79)
P80			+								(P80)
P81				+V					+	+	(P81)
P82		+	+						+		(P82)
P83		+	+						+	+	(P83)
P84									+		(P84)
P85		+							+		(P85)
P86		+							+		(P86)
P87									+		(P87)
P88		+							+	+	(P88)

Questions in MS 16 F II which are also found in the early printed editions published by Klein

(1) *Les Adevineaux amoureux* (?Paris, *c.* 1479): contains 29 verse and 71 prose questions:

V: 1–18

P: 1, 3, 6–7, 10–12, 13 (verse), 16–19, 24, 26–27, 35, 37–39, 41, 43, 47, 50, 55, 64, 71, 79, 81–83

(2) *Les Demandes d'amours* (Lyon, *c.* 1530): contains 45 verse and 31 prose questions:

V: 1, 3 (prose), 5–8, 9 (prose), 10, 14 (prose), 16

P: 1–2, 4–5, 23, 47, 52, 54–55, 62, 67, 69–70, 73–76, 79–80, 82

(3) *Demandes et responces d'amours* (Paris, 1526; once attributed to Alain Chartier): contains 43 verse questions:

V: 7–9, 10 (prose), 11–12, 14, 16

www.ingramcontent.com/pod-product-compliance
Ingram Content Group UK Ltd.
Pitfield, Milton Keynes, MK11 3LW, UK
UKHW042008190726
13854UKWH00005B/2215

9 780907 570097